Falling Into The Big L

Love and Sexuality on the Way to Adulthood

Falling Into The Big L

Love and Sexuality on the Way to Adulthood

KAREN J. SANDVIG

Regal Books
A Division of GL Publications
Ventura, California, U.S.A.

Published by Regal Books
A Division of GL Publications
Ventura, California 93006
Printed in U.S.A.

Library of Congress Cataloging-in-Publication Data applied for

1 2 3 4 5 6 7 8 9 10 / 91 90 89

With all my love,
to Douglas, my partner in life. And to Matt and Luke and the women who will someday be their partners in life!

1 Corinthians 1:4

Contents

A Personal Letter from the Author

Dear Teen:

I hope you'll read this book. I've written it to help you through the last part of your passage into adulthood. Things can get so confusing in today's world that it takes much of the fun out of growing up. That makes me very sad. You should be able to enjoy this stage of your life without having to worry about things all the time.

I'm not going to preach at you. I only want to share several examples of what's going on in the lives of many teens just like you today and tell you about some of the great things life has in store for you! I want you to see many of the different ways that other kids are handling their choices—good and bad. This may help you to know that you're not alone with the pressures of finishing your growing up, and also to help you sort out your feelings about a lot of the tough issues you face.

In this book I talk about your sexuality and having healthy couple relationships. I can't think of anything more important to your future right now than these. You can go to college at any age; as an adult; you can start businesses or careers whenever you want; in a few years you won't have curfews or house rules set for you by anyone but you, and soon there won't be laws preventing you from voting, drinking, or the like. But if you get pregnant, diseased, or unhappily married, your life for the next several years may become like climbing a very steep mountain when you could be walking easily over the ups and downs of a gently rolling meadow.

Some of the kids in the book may seem "too good to be true," or maybe their parents appear to be left over from the "Leave It to Beaver" era. Sometimes you may feel like, "Yeah, right! This is great, but my parents spend more time on their own dates than home with me and I've been getting it on with my partner for three years already. This stuff isn't for me!"

Wrong. It *is* for you! You *can* lay the groundwork for a healthy, happy, loving family life of your own! By seeing both good ways and bad ways that people handle themselves you can make your own choices more confidently. Always remember that you *do* have a choice when it comes to your sexuality and relationships! Your choices belong to you and nobody else!

It's good to date and get comfortable with yourself. To this day, spearmint-flavored gum reminds me of my first kiss. Certain songs still make my heart jump and fill up with the love I had for my guy when I was a teenager—and I've been married to him for more than a decade!

I was a rebellious teen. I was a teenage mother. I've had some very real mountains to climb in my life. Thankfully, I've also been able to let God lead me safely up the rocky paths and I'm a better, stronger, more blessed person because of it.

I will be mentioning God in this book—not as a sermon but as a part of life to consider. I can't bring up all the other areas of your life without bringing up God. If it bothers you, skip the parts that talk about Him. Or you can just read right through them. Don't worry, they won't rub off on you if you don't want them to.

One of the things that concerns me about your growing up in today's world is that you're seldom taught what "normal" family life is all about, or given skills to develop real intimacy, or shown how to respect yourself and your dating partner, or tutored in the fine art of handling attraction to the opposite sex. At times you're not even told *how* to do many of the things that adults seems to want you to do—such as set goals, have relationships that set you free, and deal with peer pressure (just saying no is a little too simple sometimes, isn't it?). And who tells you what to do if you *do* mess up big time? Who do you ask about your fears regarding homosexuality without having them think you're gay?

These are some of the things I'll talk about in this book. You'll get to know how others confront and cope with the problems of teen sexuality today—the whole person, not just the dissected pieces. I highlight questions that concern real teenagers, ages 14 to 19, and I offer answers to these questions, as well as guidance to help you work through the difficult struggles of your teen years.

Quizzes at the end of each chapter may help you evaluate where you are right now in regard to many issues that surround your growing up. Use them to start discussions or enhance your thoughts on how to cope with the challenges you may be facing in your life.

For example, your sexuality is a *good gift from God!* First Timothy 4:4 says, "Everything [not *some* things, but *everything*!] God created is good, and nothing is to be rejected." Some people shy away from mixing Christianity and sexuality, but sexuality is a part of us which God created, so we know that our sexuality is good! We mature sexually just as we do physically, mentally, emotionally, and spiritually. It is up to each one of us to make choices regarding our sexuality and to live with the consequences.

For some, this book may seem too simple. For those who are living with physical and emotional beatings, incest, prostitution, or other painful things—I know you're there. I'd like to reach each and every one of you. I can't address all problems in a few pages. But, I speak about many of them. And I promise you that there is relief for your pain. There is hope for your life! There are people who care and places you can go for help right now, today, listed throughout the book. At the end, there is a special list that tells "Where to Get Help" if you need it. Please call one of the numbers if you need guidance! You are the only one who can make the move to seek help for the final part of your passage into adulthood!

We start right off with a short quiz so you can see how informed you are about a few of the more factual things that have to do with your sexuality. As with all the quizzes, use the information to spark thought, discussion and consideration. There are very few topics that have "absolute" answers. You must put each suggestion or example offered throughout the book into your own personal circumstances before you decide that anything is right or wrong for you.

If I could have only one wish for all of you who read the following chapters, it's that you'll find the love, goodness, and fulfillment in life that I've been blessed with in mine! The best part of this wish is that I know it *can* come true if you'll let it!

God Bless,

Karen

Beginning Quiz

Do you know what is fact and what is fiction regarding your sexuality?

Answer the following as True or False:

1. A girl can't get pregnant the first time she and her partner have sexual relations. **T F**

2. A person can only get infected with AIDS if he/she is a homosexual or intravenous drug user. **T F**

3. Incest is when one family member sexually molests another member of the family besides his/her spouse (this includes forced sexual intercourse). **T F**

4. If adult-teen rape or incest occurs, it's usually the teenage girl or boy who has seduced the adult. **T F**

5. The only way to really prove I love my partner is to have a sexual relationship. **T F**

6. It is common for teenage boys to experience some breast growth during adolescence. **T F**

7. Teenagers are actually miniature adults. **T F**

8. God disapproves of sex. **T F**

9. Drinking alcohol will not affect whether I decide to have sex with someone and it won't bother my performance. **T F**

10. A girl cannot get pregnant during her period. **T F**

11. It is normal for adolescent boys to have nocturnal emissions (wet dreams). **T F**

12. Teenage girls cannot experience Pre-Menstrual Syndrome (PMS). **T F**

13. If an adult says or does something, it must be right. **T F**

14. Even if a guy "pulls out" before he ejaculates, the girl may still get pregnant. **T F**

15. If a girl stands up right after having sex, the sperm will not be able to swim "upstream" to fertilize an egg (ovum), so she can't get pregnant. **T F**

Tally Up!

1. False: A girl can get pregnant the first, third, or fortieth time she has sex! Sperm and eggs that are ready to be fertilized do not keep track of how many times a couple has sex. There are *no* exceptions to the rule. It *can* happen to you!

2. False: AIDS (Acquired Immunodeficiency Syndrome) is a virus. It can live in a human body for long periods of time, even years, before symptoms appear. A person can become infected with the AIDS virus by behaving in the following risky ways:

   a. Having unprotected sex (without a condom) with an infected person
   b. Having sex with someone you don't know well
   c. Having sex with someone who has been with several partners
   d. Having sex with several partners
   e. Having vaginal and oral sex with someone who shoots drugs or engages in anal sex
   f. Shooting drugs/sharing drug needles and syringes
   g. Having anal sex with or without a condom.

A person can help guard against becoming infected with the AIDS virus by behaving in the following safe ways:

   a. Not shooting drugs
   b. Not having sex at all
   c. Having sex with one, mutually faithful, uninfected partner.

The above information was taken from a brochure that the U.S. Department of Health and Human Services published in 1988. The department encourages the public to utilize it. If you would like a copy of the entire brochure write to:

Public Health Service Centers for Disease Control
P.O. Box 6003
Rockville, MD 20850

3. True: Incest is a frightening topic for many people. It is sick behavior, and its victims are tragically in the path of a relative who is abusing them horribly. If you have been forced to have sex with a relative, or been touched in a way that is sexual, do not wait—get to someone for help. You may want to call one of the "Help" numbers at the end of this book. Or look up a counselor, pastor, or social service agency in your phone book. Ask a teacher, a trusted friend, or coach for help. The person who is molesting you is very sick. He/she needs to be exposed and stopped. You deserve help to get over the terrible trauma which you have experienced!

4. False: One way a person who rapes or commits incest may try to control the one whom he/she is abusing is by trying to make the victim believe (either by words or actions) that he/she is somehow responsible for what's happening. A male relative may try to convince a young girl that she has come on to him and it's her fault he abused her. A female relative may try to force a boy to keep quiet about incest by blaming him for her sickness. It just isn't true—you are *not* responsible! You do *not* deserve such treatment! There is nothing in the world that you could do that would justify someone abusing you. Please believe me. Get to someone who will help you stop the abuse and work through this horror-filled situation. You can get through it and live a full, happy life.

It must be pointed out that hugging, kissing, holding hands, or other gestures of affection by family and friends is *not* sexual molestation or abuse! They are a normal, healthy, important part of showing love and care.

5. False: If someone tries to force you into *proving* your love by pushing you to do something you don't want to do, then chances are that person doesn't really love you at all. Sex is a personal, very private aspect of a healthy marriage. Your mind, body, and soul belong to you. If your partner really loves you he/she will want to help build you up and respect your wishes just as you want to do for a partner you truly love. If a partner *has* forced you to have sex against your will, you are

the victim of date rape. Tell an adult who can help you, just as you would with any other sexual abuse. You are not alone! Date rape happens to many fine young people, and you can work through the trauma!

6. True: It is usual for adolescent boys to develop breast tissue. Sometimes your breasts may be tender or painful. This generally does not indicate any underlying hormone trouble, but it never hurts to check with your physician. The breasts may be back to normal in a few months, or they may stay swollen for a couple of years, depending on the individual.

7. False: Teenagers are *not* the same as adults! You are still growing up and learning how to be adults. You will probably never go through such a rapid change in your physical, mental, and emotional development again. Try to understand that you still need the guidance of adults to help you through this final phase of your passage into adulthood. You may feel restricted and think you should be treated as an adult, but this simply is not true—you need time to let your basic adult traits settle into your personality. Meanwhile, try to relax and enjoy the freedoms you do have!

8. False: God sanctions sex! It is a gift from Him and He wants a husband and wife to fully relax, enjoy, and appreciate their sexuality together.

9. False: Alcohol tends to destroy normal self-control. Therefore, people often do things they wouldn't think of doing while they were sober. No one—and I mean no one—is bigger or stronger than the bottle! Alcohol is actually a depressant. It commonly brings people down, makes them feel tired, dulls their senses, and can make guys impotent while they're under the influence.

10. False: A girl's menstrual cycle can be a very sensitive thing. She may ovulate in the middle of her cycle one month, twice the next and not at all the next. There is no time during any woman's menstrual cycle when she is absolutely safe from becoming pregnant!

11. True: It is common for adolescent boys to wake up in

the middle of the night or early in the morning to find that they have ejaculated. This may happen only a few times or several, and is usually nothing to worry about and certainly nothing to be ashamed of.

12. False: Any menstruating female can suffer the bloating, irritability, nausea, pain, cramps, or any other symptoms that may be associated with the few days before the onset of a period. If you are vulnerable to PMS symptoms you may want to see your physician for an examination and to discuss ways to minimize the discomfort.

13. False: Not every adult has it together by any means. You must develop and learn to use skills that will help you to determine if an adult is worthy of your trust, respect, and loyalty. Some danger signs to watch for are:

a. Adults who are very secretive and don't want you to discuss with anyone else what they tell you
b. Adults who are involved in immoral or criminal behavior
c. Those who don't hesitate to expose you to immoral or illegal activities
d. Anyone who tries to encourage you to participate in anything that is directly against your rules, values or beliefs
e. Those who are fanatical or extreme about anything
f. Anybody you feel uncomfortable with, especially if it's "just a feeling" you have.

14. True: Even before ejaculation there is usually a discharge of fluid containing sperm. If this sperm has even come close to the opening of the vagina it is possible for it to make its way up the vaginal canal to an egg that may just be ready for fertilization.

15. False: Sperm are pretty hardy little fellows. A girl can stand up, douche, or run laps, but if the sperm has had a chance to reach the vaginal canal it may swim its way right up to a waiting egg.

In the first chapter we'll look at the great power and pleasures that come with being attracted to the opposite sex. Anyone who has ever been in love knows the excitement and energy this experience offers. Let's explore the dynamics of a relationship from its beginning and look at how differently males and females see each other.

CHAPTER ONE

Now *There's* a Fine Lookin' Item!

Are there really differences in the ways boys and girls react to each other and interpret each other's signals? You bet there are! You can best prepare yourself for a healthy couple relationship by learning to understand the differences *right now.* This may save you years of disappointment and insecurity!

The teacher of a ninth grade class at Huntington Park High School in California, asked her students what attractions they looked for in the opposite sex.

The boys looked for 15 physical traits and two personality traits. They wanted their women to have things like nice breasts, thighs, and rear ends.

The girls looked for 26 personality traits and only four physical ones. They wanted their men to be sensitive, have a good sense of humor, and treat them considerately.[1]

As you can see, there are exactly opposite reactions from

each sex—just like the positive and negative poles of batteries and magnets.

Before you get superiority complexes, girls, thinking guys are shallow and only care about how the package is wrapped, stop and realize this: That's just the way the guy feels at *this* stage of the game! For now, if a guy is first attracted to your figure, be flattered; it doesn't mean he doesn't like your personality too.

And guys, don't get all huffy about girls wanting you for your mind instead of those muscles you've worked so hard at building. She likes your physique, but she also loves the fact that you cared enough to spend most of your paycheck on roses and tickets to a concert for a date.

Differences don't have to mean one way is good and the other is bad. They can mean each way is half of a total picture.

Isn't it great that one half isn't complete without the other? It's great because—male and female—we need each other. Granted, there are those who never feel the need to be married, which is wonderful for them. But millions of other people want to be one-half of a healthy, sexual couple.

Knowing while you're still a teen that there can be big differences in the way males and females think about each other can give you an edge on developing healthy couple relationships. For example, a hug may mean security, comfort and love to a girl, yet be pure sexual stimulation to a guy. A girl may interpret a deep tongue-probing kiss to be a guy's seal of approval of and loyalty to her, where the guy takes it as a signal to go for it! If you are aware of the differences between the sexes, you can take care to enhance your relationships while you steer away from trouble. What can guys and girls do to be more interesting?

Any girl can be careful of her appearance and grooming and make the most of it. I can picture some of you saying, "Give me a break! I'm overweight, I have acne, and besides, I'm a Women's Libber—I'm not playing those sexist games!"

First of all, being a little overweight isn't always so bad. Not every boy appreciates a thin, gaunt figure. Believe it or not, there are a lot of guys who are afraid of a girl who is so skinny she looks downright breakable. Many guys like a little more roundness in the female figure.

Next, acne is acne, scars are scars, and if *all* a guy looks at is physical, then he *is* pretty shallow—stay away from him! There is no such thing as perfection, most often it's a matter of preference. My idea of perfection may be your idea of a losing proposition. Clean, well-groomed and tastefully dressed—that's what really counts.

Finally, liberated lady, you've heard stories about the kind of a girl a guy will take to Lover's Point—but not home to meet his parents. When you're married you can be *both* kinds of woman to your man! That's not betraying your liberation—it's making the most out of the exciting world you live in and the whole person that you are.

Ladies, one way to clear up misunderstandings about differences, is to tell you guy what you're thinking and feeling. "I want to hug and kiss, but that's not a signal I want to have sex. I'm not a teaser, I just want to be close without you getting all mad when I won't go all the way!" Or, "I feel so safe and loved when I'm in your arms, but I don't want you to take that to mean I want sex." These are considerate, loving and truthful statements that explain how you feel as a girl. You may be surprised how much a guy respects that.

You guys can brighten a relationship by being honest, sensitive, and complimentary. Telling a girl that you think she's attractive, but keeping your hands to yourself, lets her know she's with a special kind of guy. Avoiding situations that could take you too far tells her that she should take a little care in the signals she sends you. Don't tell a girl you love her if you don't. Show respect by not bragging or exaggerating to other guys about your relationship with her.

Guys, you can add oceans of depth to your couple relationships by being on time for dates, being careful about your personal appearance, telling your girl she looks or smells

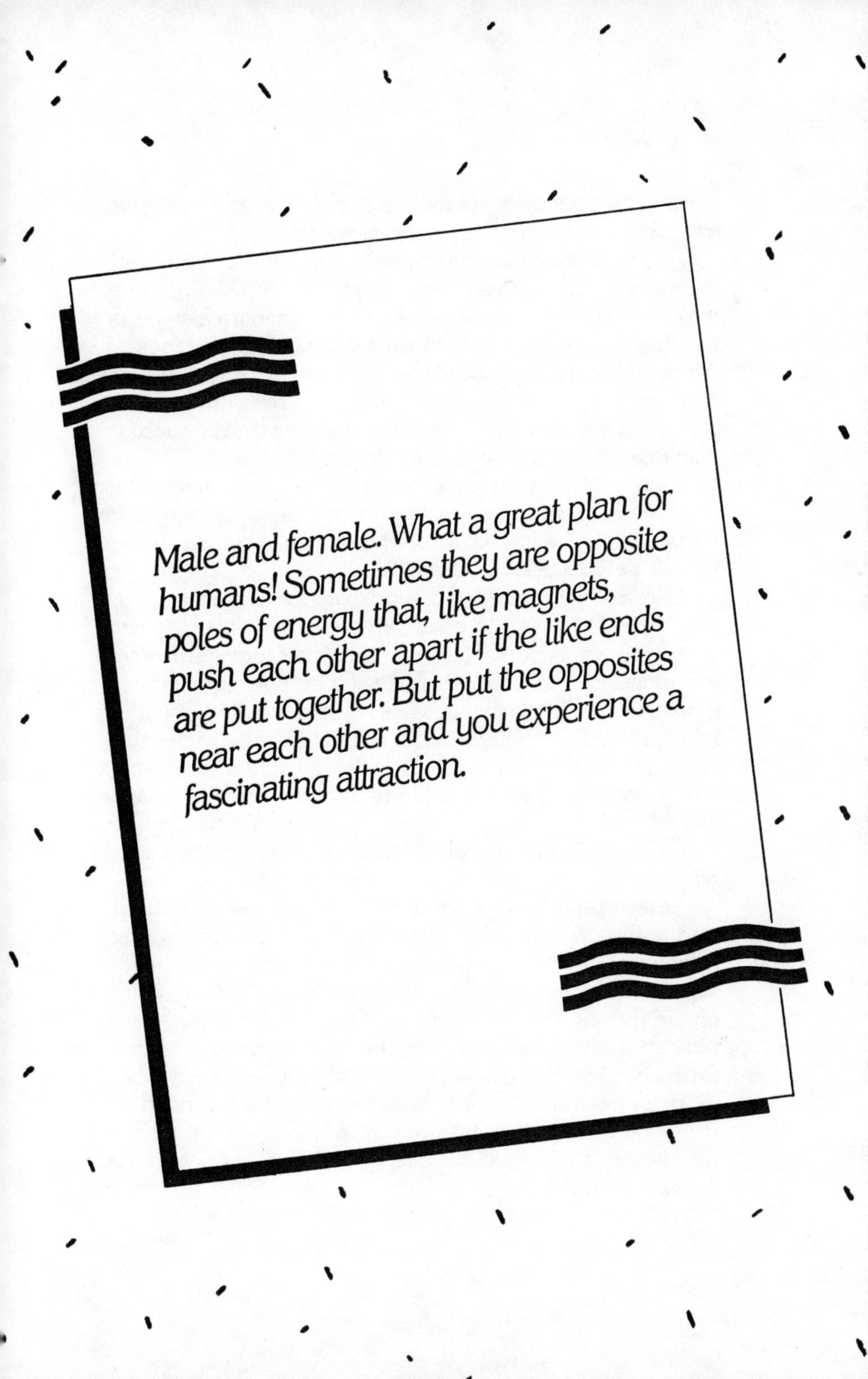

Male and female. What a great plan for humans! Sometimes they are opposite poles of energy that, like magnets, push each other apart if the like ends are put together. But put the opposites near each other and you experience a fascinating attraction.

good, calling her ahead of time to ask her out, and taking her hand while waiting in line for the movies.

Don't feel that you don't measure up because you aren't the school's "awesomest dude." A girl is more likely to pick the guy who tells her he feels bad for her when her parents or a girlfriend dumps on her, than she is the jock who stands on the corner with the guys and tosses his letter jacket at her feet.

A girl is much more likely to fall head over heals in love with the hunk who will bend down to hear a child's question than one who says, "Aw—speak up you little brat!"

A guy who has the guts to reach out for his potential is much more attractive to most girls than the "tough" guy who is willing to let his life slip away while he hides his insecurities behind a can of beer and dirty jokes.

Male and female. What a great plan for humans! Sometimes they are opposite poles of energy that, like magnets, push each other apart if the like ends are put together. But put the opposites near each other and you experience a fascinating attraction. Touch two positive sides of a battery together in a flashlight and you get zilch. But put positive to negative and, with a big enough charge, you could light up the world. *That's* what being attracted to the opposite sex in a healthy way can do!

Let's look in on one couple's relationship from the beginning and see if you identify with their example.

Sixteen-year-old Chelsea looked around the group huddled at the campfire, classmates from high school who had helped their teacher, Betsy, instruct an art class for the handicapped. Betsy had promised these six kids a special outing toward the end of the school year. And here they were, after a wonderful day at the lake, letting the warm campfire melt their experience into the treasure chest of high school memories.

Betsy interrupted the camaraderie when it was time to go. Everyone helped pack up the van. Betsy drove the kids to their homes and they all said sleepy goodnights; Chelsea was the last one out.

"Bye, Chelsea," Betsy smiled, "see you next week."

"Okay. Thanks for today, Betsy, it was such fun!" Chelsea said sincerely.

Chelsea's mother, Nan, greeted her at the front door, "Hi, honey, how'd it go?"

"Great," Chelsea responded happily. "We floated on the lake on air mattresses, rented paddle boats, swam, and roasted hot dogs over the fire tonight."

"I'm glad you had fun, Chels." Nan kissed her daughter on the forehead. "Now you'd better get to bed—you must be exhausted."

Chelsea was snuggled under her covers minutes later, gazing out the skylight over her bed at a nearly full moon. Tired as she was, her mind was full of rambling thoughts of one of the other kids who'd been at the lake today—Greg Roberts. She hardly knew Greg because they had helped out in Betsy's art class on different days throughout the year. They passed each other in the halls of their large high school between classes, and Chelsea saw him off-and-on at athletic events, dances and in the cafeteria. Today was the first time they'd ever been in the same place for any length of time. And there was something about him—something that set Chelsea's senses on edge. Not in a bad way, or a specifically good way, but in a curiously alert way. She'd watched Greg all afternoon with two other boys as they dove off the rock, swam out to where the girls lay on air mattresses, or paddled boats around the lake. Chelsea's stomach turned over even now as she remembered how Greg's muscles rippled. She drifted off to sleep thinking about his wide, attractive smile and handsome face.

The next day was Sunday. Chelsea spent it quietly reading and daydreaming. Thoughts of Greg came to her often and she began to make plans to find out more about this gorgeous hunk.

Monday morning Chelsea chose her clothing and put on her make-up with great care. She decided to ask her friend, Elizabeth, to get more information about Greg for her, because Elizabeth dated Ross, one of Greg's older brother's good friends. Chelsea grabbed a warm muffin, a glass of milk, and some bacon for breakfast and then waved good-bye to her parents. Nan thought that her pretty daughter seemed especially bright-eyed for a Monday morning.

Elizabeth was a wealth of information about Greg later that week. She told Chelsea that he was college-bound, wanting to become some sort of marketing consultant, and geared his classes toward this end. That explained why he and Chelsea weren't taking any of the same junior year courses. Chelsea was also planning to go to college but she wanted to be a botanist and was laden with a science-oriented workload.

Elizabeth took Chelsea aside at lunch and gushed, "Ooh, Chels, Greg is a real find! You know, I never paid any attention before. Since Ross is a college freshman we don't usually travel in the same circles as Greg. But I told Ross that a friend of mine was interested in Greg and asked him what the deal was."

"Elizabeth!" Chelsea said quickly. "You didn't tell Ross it was me did you? I'd die if Greg knew I was checking him out!"

"Of course not, silly!" Elizabeth tossed her long hair back over her shoulder. "Anyway, listen up, this is great news for you, Chelsea! Greg was going with some sophomore all winter and they just broke up last month. Maybe he didn't want to take her to the prom!" Elizabeth giggled.

"Elizabeth, you're terrible," Chelsea chided her feisty friend.

"Well, anyway, for the last few weeks he's been hanging out more with his buddies. They're the track and field jocks you know."

"Um-hm," Chelsea nodded as she bit into a ripe strawberry.

"Greg's on the honor roll, he has a great car and his parents evidently aren't hurting for money. They live on 'The Hill' and have a nice cabin on the lake. I was out there once to pick Ross up. And Greg is so-o cute!"

"Tell me about it!" Chelsea grinned. "I can't believe I never looked closer before!"

"Here's what you do," Elizabeth leaned toward Chelsea conspiratively. "Ross and I are going to the cabin next weekend. Greg's family throws a big Memorial Day barbecue every year, I guess. Ross said I should ask my 'friend' to come along with us and hang out."

"Oh, I couldn't!" Chelsea exclaimed. "Greg will probably have a date there. I'd be so embarrassed!"

"No, no," Elizabeth assured. "Greg and his buddies are lining up a volleyball game and water skiing runs for a whole group—the more the merrier. He'll just think you came with me to keep me company."

Chelsea thought she should probably say no, but she couldn't resist the opportunity to observe Greg more closely. The fact that it was on his own turf was an added bonus. "Okay!" she nodded her head. "I'll go! Thanks, Elizabeth!"

The next week seemed to drag and fly by all at once. Chelsea ran into some resistance from her parents about being gone on Memorial Day, as they had their own picnic planned with relatives coming for lunch. Chelsea quickly pointed out that she could see the relatives and visit a little because she didn't have to leave until after lunch. Even though Chelsea wouldn't say why the barbecue was so important to her, Nan suspected it had something to do with a boy. And Nan knew the Roberts family had a solid reputation in their community, so, in the end, she gave Chelsea permission to go.

Chelsea woke up very early on the morning of Memorial Day. She showered and dressed before her parents were even awake, which was most unusual. Nan found Chelsea at the breakfast table when she came in to make coffee and *knew* the barbecue had to have something to do with a boy. Mother and daughter chatted away until the sun began to warm them through the east windows that surrounded their breakfast nook. Nan went off to prepare for the company, and Chelsea wandered out to the back lawn.

Chelsea's father, Gary, was cleaning up around the patio. "Hi, sweetie," he greeted her. "You're up and around pretty early today!"

"Yeah," Chelsea couldn't help splitting into a grin. "I guess it's just too nice a day to miss!"

"Hmm," Gary looked curiously at her. "Since when does that get you up with the birds?"

"Oh, I don't know, Dad," Chelsea shrugged. "I'm just in a good mood, okay?"

"Okay," Gary answered. Inside he also strongly suspected the cause for Chelsea's good mood was a boy.

The hours between breakfast, lunch, and leaving for the barbecue went so slowly Chelsea thought she could've measured the seconds ticking away by a turtle's footsteps. But finally Elizabeth was at the door and Chelsea was bouncing down the sidewalk. She felt as light as a helium balloon. Ross drove out of town and toward the lake while the three made small talk. Elizabeth and Chelsea exchanged excited smiles throughout the half-hour ride.

They parked in front of a beautiful home that Chelsea hardly labeled a "cabin." She began to get butterflies in her stomach as they walked up a cobblestone path to the front door. *Maybe I'm out of my league here,* Chelsea thought.

Her anxiety lessened somewhat, however, as David greeted her warmly and said he was glad she could come to the family's annual event. Mr. and Mrs. Roberts were equally charming when David introduced her. "Chelsea is in Greg's class at school," he said.

"How nice to meet you, Chelsea," Mrs. Roberts extended her hand. "We're happy to have you. The more the better around here!"

"That goes for me too," Mr. Roberts smiled. "You make yourself right at home!"

The teens then made their way through a large family room and a perfect kitchen and onto a spacious cedar deck that overlooked a calm, tree-sheltered cove of the lake. Chelsea looked over the deck railing onto a group of adults gathering around an open barbecue pit. There was another group, however, that grabbed her attention—the teenagers playing volleyball past the lawn, near the water's edge. She looked closely at the kids in action and felt a quickening of her pulse as she spotted Greg. As he prepared to serve the ball she took in his tanned body, sandy-blond hair, and tight-fitting cutoffs. Yes, she was definitely attracted to Greg Roberts.

"C'mon," David's voice broke into her thoughts. "Let's go on down. We're gonna split into groups soon. Some will stay with the volleyball and I'll take the rest out in the boat for skiing."

Elizabeth and Chelsea hung back a little as Ross and David went down the deck stairs. Elizabeth whispered quickly, "Can you believe this, Chelsea? What a set-up!"

Is it natural to feel a mixture of excitement and anxiety over being close to someone you're attracted to?

Chelsea was actually starting to feel quite anxious, "I don't know, Elizabeth, maybe I shouldn't have come along."

"What?!" Elizabeth was incredulous as she pulled Chelsea to a stop on the patio. David and Ross were already halfway across the lawn.

"Well," Chelsea said, almost apologetically, "what if Greg thinks I'm stupid and ugly? What if he asks how I got invited? I'd be so humiliated, Elizabeth!"

"Oh, Chels!" Elizabeth shook her head. "It's not that serious. Remember you're not trying to get him to marry you, you're just here to have fun and scope him out!"

"I know," Chelsea conceded. "I'm just so nervous now. I don't want to look like a fool!"

"Fool?" Elizabeth's eyes opened wide. "Chelsea, get real!

You're darling! Look at you—you're great looking, you've got a cute figure, you're smart—and to top it off, you're nice!"

"Thanks, Elizabeth. That makes me feel better. I'll try to relax a little."

"Come on, Elizabeth!" Ross hollered from the volleyball court.

The girls walked over to him. David and Greg stepped up to Ross at the same time. David put his arm around Greg's shoulder, "Girls, I think you probably know my little brother, Greg, from school." David turned to Greg, "Do you know Elizabeth and Chelsea?"

Greg smiled and looked first to Elizabeth, "I guess we haven't really met. Hello!"

"Hi!" Elizabeth responded.

Greg turned to Chelsea, his eyes locking with hers, "I know Chelsea from Betsy's art class. Hi, Chelsea, glad you could make it!"

Chelsea thought her heart stopped in that instant. She murmured a soft, "Thanks, Greg," and looked shyly at the ground.

Thankfully, David spoke up, "Well, Ross, c'mon. Let's get the first ski group going. Do you girls ski?"

Elizabeth and Chelsea both nodded. They had their swimming suits on under their shorts, and a change of clothes in the car.

"Well, you wanna come now or wait for another run?" David asked.

"Now!" Elizabeth answered right away. Chelsea hesitated. She didn't want to stay back without Elizabeth but she wanted to be with the group Greg was in, too. Ross made the decision for her.

He said, "Elizabeth, why don't you come now and Chelsea can go when Greg takes his group out. Is that all right with you, Chelsea?"

"Sure." Chelsea said. "Yeah, I'll stay and play volleyball."

David, Ross, and Elizabeth went on their way with a few

others down to the boat dock. Greg said, "Let's go! Do you want to be on my team?"

"Yes," Chelsea smiled, "but you may be sorry. I'm not the best volleyball player in the world."

"That's okay," Greg replied. "We're just out to have a good time."

Chelsea was soon too busy playing the game to be very self-conscious. Both teams were co-ed and friendly. Chelsea knew some of the other kids. She felt at ease and thoroughly enjoyed herself.

By the time the first group of skiers came back she was feeling a real part of the celebration. She went with Greg's team down to the dock and scrambled into the boat for their turn at skiing. Chelsea sat behind and opposite Greg, who was driving. His best friend, Todd, was in the front passenger seat to be a spotter for the skiers.

Two-by-two the teens took their turns being pulled behind the boat. From where she sat, Chelsea could discreetly watch Greg as he skillfully maneuvered the boat. He was so awesome! Chelsea thought he was absolutely adorable and decided that she would burst into ecstasy if Greg ever asked her out on a date alone. When it was Todd's turn to ski, Greg turned to Chelsea.

"Wanna come up and spot?" he asked.

"Sure." Chelsea said enthusiastically. She stood up to step between the front seats and her bare thigh brushed against Greg's arm. Chelsea felt an electrical impulse zing through her as their limbs touched. Greg's skin was warm from the afternoon sun. Chelsea tried to appear nonchalant, "Excuse me, tight fit."

"Hey, that's okay," Greg answered. "Do you know what to do?"

"Yup."

"All right. Ready, Todd?!" Greg shouted.

"Yeah! We're ready!" Todd called back.

And they were off. Chelsea was thrilled to be so near Greg

with wind blowing at her back as she watched the two skiers. For those few minutes she fantasized that she and Greg were a couple within the group and it was wonderful! Then Greg and Chelsea were the only two who hadn't skied and it was time to take their turn.

Chelsea pulled her shirt and shorts off. As she straightened up she caught Greg watching her intently and felt a blush come to her cheeks. Greg turned away quickly and rolled over the side of the boat to put on his slalom ski. Chelsea hopped into the water on the opposite side where her ski floated. They paddled along their separate ski ropes until they could grab the ends and get into a ready position.

Chelsea smiled at Greg, "I'm glad I came today. I'm really having fun."

Greg looked at her and said seriously, "I'm glad you came, too, Chelsea."

Todd shouted back then, asking if they were ready. Greg signaled with his arm and they were up skiing in seconds. Chelsea was so happy she couldn't believe it. She felt as though Greg's words had held more meaning than if he'd been talking to one of the guys, and this gave her hope that maybe they could get to know each other better.

They took turns criss-crossing over the wake on their skis and grinning at each other. They laughed when one or the other had to catch their balance and Chelsea wished they could keep going forever. It seemed only seconds before Greg signaled for them to throw their handbars up and drop into the water. They took their skis off and dog-paddled while Todd circled around in the boat to pick them up.

Chelsea fell into her seat pleasantly exhausted and wrapped herself in a towel. Greg took the wheel and headed back to shore so that the next group could go out skiing. Chelsea cherished the last hour she'd been close to Greg and thought she'd never forget it.

Elizabeth rushed to her as Chelsea walked up from the dock, "Chels! How'd it go? Did you have fun? Did Greg notice you?" she asked in a low, excited voice.

"Elizabeth," Chelsea looked around before continuing, making sure no one else could hear. "He's so cool! We skied double and I caught him really looking at me just before we went in to ski!"

"All right!" Elizabeth threw her arm around Chelsea's shoulder. "You're on your way! And get this! A band is going to start playing at dark! A real dance—right here by the lake, under the stars and a full moon! Can you even think of anything sexier?"

"Oh, Elizabeth! Stop it!" Chelsea rolled her eyes. "You get so carried away!"

Inside, though, Chelsea was full of hopeful anticipation. Maybe she could even dance with Greg! Her spine tingled as she thought of the possibility. She and Elizabeth went to get their change of clothes from Ross's car. Since the house was teeming with activity downstairs, Mrs. Roberts directed the girls upstairs to her bedroom.

"She is so nice!" Elizabeth spouted. "What a doll! And look at this room!"

Chelsea gazed around the immaculately decorated suite. It looked like a scene right out of a decorating magazine. Chelsea walked across the room and opened a door into a bathroom that would be any teenage girl's dream. "Elizabeth," Chelsea breathed, "look at this. A sunken spa, mirrored walls, Spanish tiles and towels thicker than my bedspread!"

"Ooh!" Elizabeth rushed past Chelsea and down the steps into the spa, "I tell you, girl, I think I could fall in love with Greg's family and life-style even if I wasn't in love with him!"

Elizabeth's statement was like a cold rag slapped on Chelsea's warm face. "Elizabeth," she scolded, "you're being ridiculous! It's one thing to admire someone's life-style, but to compare that to loving the person is *sick*!"

"Oh, Chelsea," Elizabeth tried to sound cynical, "you're such a baby! Don't you know anything about the real world?"

Chelsea felt a little sheepish for coming down on Elizabeth. After all this was just a holiday barbecue and Elizabeth was only kidding. "Sorry, I guess I got carried away myself," she said.

"Aw, c'mon, Chels," Elizabeth said, "it's okay. You just need to lighten up a little."

The girls changed clothes, combed their hair, re-did their make-up and delighted in posing in front of the mirrors. When they thought they'd been gone from the party long enough, and decided they were as pretty as they were going to get for the evening, they skipped down the stairs and out to the patio where most everyone was already in line with plates to get their food. Elizabeth and Chelsea did likewise.

Is it "normal" to feel threatened when someone you're attracted to is with another person?

Chelsea was leaning over to say something to Elizabeth when she happened to see Greg at the edge of the crowd—laughing with a very attractive blonde. She got a sinking sensation in her stomach, as she watched Greg put his arm loosely around the girl's waist and walk with her toward the boat dock in the gathering dusk. They climbed into the boat and just sat there. Chelsea felt as if the breath were squeezed right out of her and she wished more than anything at that moment that she was the girl with Greg. At the same time she felt jealous resentment toward the blonde. Then she felt silly. Of course, girls who were much more outgoing, more confident and prettier than she was would be after Greg's attention. Who was she trying to kid?

One saving grace was that Greg didn't know how attracted Chelsea was to him. Elizabeth had not noticed Greg and his female companion. She and Chelsea took their plates and walked around until they saw Ross, David, and a couple of others at a picnic table. They went over and sat down. Ross seemed so pleased to see Elizabeth that Chelsea felt a small tug of envy, but she quickly squelched it and told herself that she was being very selfish.

Chelsea mostly picked at her food and pushed it around her plate. Her feeling of rejection caused her to begin looking at each young girl who walked by and evaluate them as being prettier or better proportioned than she was. Darkness began to caress the people milling around. Before it could totally envelop them, however, a full, bursting moon rose to spotlight the party.

The band struck up their first tune. Chelsea's feet tapped in time to the music despite the personal disappointment she felt. By the third song, Ross was pulling Elizabeth up to dance and David asked Chelsea if she would.

"C'mon, little one, you look like you could use some new spark. Let's dance."

Chelsea accepted David's hand gratefully. She had just been wondering if she would sit at the picnic table all evening while everyone else enjoyed the music. Chelsea and David danced their way through the next two songs.

As the next song began Greg and the blonde slipped in beside them and danced, too. Chelsea felt her face flush and she became very self-conscious of her movements. She couldn't keep from looking over at the girl dancing with Greg.

David, two years older and perceptive for his age, thought that he was going to have to intervene before Chelsea gave up on Greg completely. He watched the expressions play openly on her face and felt empathy for her. She was really cute and seemed like a nice girl. He liked what he knew of her and what Ross had told him about her. But he also knew his brother. If things were left up to Greg, Chelsea and he would probably never get past saying hello in the halls at school.

Greg, however, shocked both David and Chelsea as the song they'd been dancing to ended. He grabbed David's arm and said, "Hey, big brother, why don't you take our dear cousin off my hands and switch dance partners with me?"

Chelsea thought her chin must have dropped to her chest. Cousin? The blonde was their cousin! Chelsea's heart sang with a renewed joy. David grinned widely and said heartily, "My pleasure!"

Chelsea stood stock still until David nudged her softly toward Greg. She smiled her thanks at David and her acceptance to Greg. The band struck up a fast rock 'n' roll tune. The evening reverberated with the beat and Chelsea's whole body swayed with it. All her senses were so keen that they took on lives of their own. The smell of the cool, damp air tickled her lungs. The concrete under her feet felt more like a thick cloud. The taste of her cherry lip-gloss was sweet on her tongue. The sound of the music filled her ears with an echo that she thought would always remind her of this night. And the sight of Greg dancing before her—with her—gave her such a deep sense of well-being that she was completely overwhelmed.

The song ended and Greg placed a hand lightly on her arm, "Thanks, Chelsea."

Chelsea didn't know whether they would dance again or not. She desperately hoped so. The band began to play a slow, romantic tune and Chelsea stood holding her breath. Greg took the initiative once more. He pulled her gently into his arms.

Chelsea went into Greg's arms with magnetic force. She vowed to remember forever the softness of his flannel shirt, the scent of his cologne, and the warmth of his body. To Chelsea's amazement Greg leaned his mouth down to her ear and whispered, "I wanted us to be together like this ever since that night around the campfire with Betsy and the others."

Chelsea pulled back to look deep into Greg's eyes. They were navy blue pools of liquid emotion and she knew he was sincere. She lay her head into the crook of his neck and said huskily, "Me too."

He hugged her tightly, she hugged him back, and all was well with the world.

Can people be attracted to each other for different reasons?

Attraction to a member of the opposite sex can be a magnificent, powerful thing. Like gifts piled high under a Christmas tree, attraction can also come in all shapes and sizes. As human beings we can be attracted to many different things about a person—his or her physical appearance, social status, material possessions, family ties, athletic performance, gentle ways, or common religious background. We can be attracted to another for reasons that we cannot possibly explain in words. Again, like Christmas packages all wrapped up in pretty paper, we may go on the instinctive, mysterious promise that something wonderful lies beneath the surface.

Attraction may very well be one of the most intensely pleasant experiences between two people. It can also cause anxiety, pain, insecurity, and despair. Thrills and excitement mixed with nervousness and wondering can be excruciatingly painful for some.

Attraction is romantic. It is unnerving. It can cause people to do seemingly crazy things such as staying up all night to be together, driving 100 miles back and forth to date someone, or changing otherwise normal behavior patterns.

Attraction to another can be a delightful, wondrous thing. It can also be too intense sometimes for our own good. Whether we are immediately and deeply attracted to someone or attracted in a growing way over a period of time, we need to know how to react to attraction and still keep our emotions from taking control of our minds and bodies.

For instance, Chelsea and Greg could have let their senses give in to temptation. The easiest reaction for most of us is to let stimulations from outside us overcome the pleasurable sensations going on inside us. Chelsea and Greg could have done the *easiest* thing and let the moon, music, mystery, movement, and mood sweep them into a private corner where they could react to their attraction for each other by having sex.

Emphasis is put on *easiest* because the easy thing is not necessarily the best thing for us. If we can appreciate that fact, then we can respect Chelsea and Greg for choosing a more difficult reaction to the strong attraction they had toward each other. They danced, admired, and enjoyed each other for the rest of the barbecue, but stayed with the group and parted that evening with a short hug.

Chelsea and Greg began to date and get to know each other better after the Memorial Day celebration. They chatted when they saw each other in the halls at school or in the cafeteria. They went to movies, studied together, and did a variety of other things as a couple. Their attraction for each other did not lessen. In fact, it grew stronger.

Chelsea's parents spoke to her frankly about her situation and the dangers of letting herself get carried away into a sexual relationship. Chelsea told them that their concerns were unnecessary. She assured them she had the strength to make the right decision for herself. Inside, however, she really did wonder if she had the strength she professed to have. Her parents each silently wondered this too and hoped very much that she did.

Can teens really control themselves in the middle of sexual tension?

The physical tension between Chelsea and Greg mounted. They were genuinely "in love." They had much in common and enjoyed their exclusive relationship. As they got further into summer they spent a lot of time at Greg's family's lake home—the romantic setting where they began as a couple. They had enough time alone together that it became extremely tough to refrain from giving in to the pressures of the loud, sexual urges that were calling from within their bodies.

One afternoon in the hot sunshine, all alone beside the lake, things started getting out of control. Innocent kissing and hugging turned into passionate fondling. They two lay on the ground entangled in each other's arms. Greg began to slip Chelsea's bikini top off. The temptation to let it happen warred with the alarm bells screaming inside Chelsea. She really did want to let things take their "natural" course. But the alarm signals were just a fraction louder than temptation—this time—and she pulled abruptly away from Greg's embrace.

He was stunned, "Hey! Chelsea! What's the matter?!"

"Greg, this is wrong! We have to stop and talk about what we're doing!"

Greg looked into Chelsea's eyes and knew that she felt genuine regret that they were not in a position where they were free to follow their passions. She was hurting. He really did love and respect her, so he pulled himself into a sitting position. "Okay, Chelsea, let's talk."

The pent-up physical and emotional frustration was too much for Chelsea to bear and she burst into tears. Greg quickly gathered her into his arms. This time it was not a sexual embrace. Greg really wanted to comfort Chelsea and she needed his support badly. They clung together for several moments until Chelsea had gotten most of her frustration out. She sat back slowly and looked at Greg, her eyes still sparkling with tears.

"That was probably one of the most unselfish things anyone has ever done for me, Greg. To put you own needs aside in order to help me sort out my feelings. I don't ever need to ask myself why I love you, because I already know!"

Chelsea and Greg talked many times after that about their sexual attraction for each other. They had long conversations about their choice not to have sexual intercourse. They did the extremely *difficult* thing to do. By choosing to meet the challenge of taking the more difficult road, Greg and Chelsea reaped some immensely valuable benefits. They experienced the following in great measure:

1. Respect for each other
2. Self-respect
3. Self-confidence
4. Trust in themselves and each other
5. Pleasure in other areas of their developing relationship
6. Love and appreciation of who they were individually and as a couple
7. Sharing their separate and mutual inner strengths
8. Freedom to enjoy the sensations of their attraction without feeling threatened or defensive.

Specific things young couples can do to help stay on the path of abstinence, and still experience the tremendous pleasures of being in love, are mentioned throughout this book. For now, we will discuss the importance of having healthy bonds in any relationship, but particularly in couple situations. It can be very difficult for two teenagers in love to nurture their relationships with each other, peers, parents, teachers, and others, while also abstaining from sex.

But God offers us His word of promise and encouragement in 1 Corinthians 10:13: "No temptation has seized you except what is common to man. And God is faithful; he will not let you be tempted beyond what you can bear. But when you are tempted, he will also provide a way out so that you can stand up under it."

This is also encouragement for those of you who are already sexually involved but want to find you way out of your circumstances. It is never too late to make anything right between you and God—*never too late*! Isaiah 1:18 promises, "Though your sins are like scarlet, they shall be as white as snow."

The powerful feelings of being attracted to a member of the opposite sex is a great pleasure to experience and be thankful for. It is also an opportunity to learn to appreciate your sexuality and still react to it in a healthy way.

Can you enjoy the pleasures of being attracted to the opposite sex without losing touch with reality?

Answer Yes or No to each item below:

1. I always notice the color of a date's eyes. **Y N**
2. I am sensitive about the way a date smells, dresses, and speaks. **Y N**
3. I dream of finding just the right mate. **Y N**
4. I believe that if I choose my mate carefully, all will be well in our world as a couple. **Y N**
5. When I'm attracted to someone of the opposite sex my body tingles, aches, and/or feels different than usual. **Y N**
6. I would never date someone again who had tried to pressure me into having sex. **Y N**
7. I've mostly gone steady with the same partner since junior high school. **Y N**
8. I date people my parents usually don't approve of. **Y N**
9. It seems that most of the people I date have serious problems at home. **Y N**
10. I often find myself in positions where I have to "back out." For example, parking with my date, lying to get out of social commitments, or having my parents tell a caller I'm not home when really I just don't want to talk. **Y N**

11. When I started dating, my grades slipped noticeably. **Y N**

12. Since I've been dating I'm thinking about not going away to college, or I'm changing other plans so I can stay close to my partner. **Y N**

13. My date's parents usually seem much easier to get along with than mine. **Y N**

14. I've had a partner break up with me because he/she felt I was getting "too serious." **Y N**

15. I'm always giving gifts to the person I'm dating. **Y N**

16. I'm self-conscious about my body when I'm on a date. I often feel too fat, too small, or "not enough" in some way. **Y N**

17. Certain songs remind me of special times I've had with dates. **Y N**

18. I definitely remember my first kiss! **Y N**

19. My steady and I try to spend every moment we can together—we don't do a lot with friends separately. **Y N**

20. I feel really jealous when someone I've dated more than once goes out with someone else. I usually get back at him/her for it. **Y N**

21. While under the influence of alcohol or recreationals drugs I have done things I usually wouldn't have done. **Y N**

22. I am feeling trapped in a relationship because I'm sexually involved and I fear being caught or never finding someone else who'll accept me if I break up with my present partner. **Y N**

23. I'm dating someone largely because my peers think he/she is really "hot." **Y N**

24. I think God is just a fairy tale people make up to explain things they don't understand. **Y N**

25. Sometimes I feel so attracted to someone I just want to let go and forget morals, rules and the future. **Y N**

Tally Up!

If you answered "yes" to 4, 6, 7, 8, 9, 10, 12, 13, 14, 15, 19, 21, 23, or 24, please stop and examine your dating and emotional style! Could it be that you're having trouble at home and you may be trying to get the support you need by clinging to a dating partner for security or as a way to find love and acceptance? Maybe you're dating an "unacceptable" kind of person to rebel against your parents or make a statement about your self-worth to peers. Maybe you're leaning on a couple relationship too hard—depending on it to shelter you from the normal growing pains of adolescence.

You cannot completely escape the challenges, confusion or conflicts of growing up. They are a part of your passage into adulthood. If you answered yes to most of the questions noted, try to find an adult you can trust or respect and immediately discuss your present dating style, emotional stability, and hopes for the future. Go to a relative, teacher, counselor, or pastor and ask for help to sort through your feelings and get directed down a healthy path of development.

If you answered "yes" to 11, 20 and/or 22, along with or apart from some of the other numbers above, please ask someone for advice. If your school work is suffering extensively because you're giving attention exclusively to a dating partner, then you will benefit greatly from reevaluating your goals and plans. This is especially important if you are hoping to attend college—it is vital that you use your best efforts toward keeping your grades up.

If you get so jealous that you're venting (and getting) revenge every time a former date goes out with someone else, then it could be that you're insecure, having problems with adjusting in relationships, or needing someone to love and accept you just the way you are.

If you are sexually active and feeling trapped, you need to free yourself. And you can! It doesn't matter what people may say or do—they don't have to live in your skin. You're the only one who has the power to change how you're living your life!

If you answered "yes" to 1, 2, 3, 5, 16, 17, 18, 25, congratulations! You are probably a healthy, sensitive, well-adjusted teenager—enjoy! Your senses are alive with the joy and excitement of being attracted to the opposite sex, but you seem to have a good bit of common sense too! And common sense is vital throughout your life.

One area where common sense can help you tremendously is in choosing your dating partners, styles, and friends. Your relationships with others can hold you back or set you free. We'll discuss how to make good choices about the people you're tied to next.

CHAPTER TWO

Ties that Hold You Back or Set You Free

Liza, 16, has dated Jake exclusively since before her 15th birthday. They have shared a lot together, including the normal ups and downs of teen life at home, school, work, and play. They've known the disappointments of not making the first-string basketball team and failing school exams. They've been together during the excitement of getting their driver's licenses and the thrill of first kisses. In many ways they have formed a deep bond between them, one that is very precious.

What does it mean to "bond" with someone? It means you enter into an agreement that bonds you together with another person for a period of time—sometimes for life, such as in a marriage agreement. We bond with others—short-term or long-term—all through our lives. We do this because we need each other. We were created that way. We all need to feel wanted, loved, and somehow connected to others.

Teens especially need to bond with others because you face making many formidable decisions when you've only been on earth approximately one-fifth of your expected lifespan. Doug Burleigh, president of Young Life, a youth ministry, points out that 20 years ago college kids were making the kinds of decisions that junior high kids must make today.[1] Nearly all of these decisions have to do with relationships—with peers, dates, parents, teachers, authorities, and acquaintances.

Any meaningful relationship requires some bonding with another person. Healthy bonding as a couple requires that both people be aware of some of the risks of *unwise* bonding. Unhealthy bonding can cause consequences that may not show up for several years.

I don't say this to take away from the special bond which teen couples form, but to make you aware that there are risks and consequences in any serious relationship that may not be immediately apparent.

Most psychologists agree that adolescence is the most difficult period in people's lives.[2] In fact, this time of life can be so difficult that as many as six million American youth suffer from clinical depression at one time or another during their teen years.[3] There were 650,000 teen suicides in 1984 and one every 90 minutes in 1986. For every one teen who dies by his own hand, three others attempt to take their lives.[4]

Otis Bowen, Secretary of Health and Human Services, notes that about 3 out of every 10 teens have real alcohol problems.[5] A 1986 study on cocaine use among high school seniors indicated that 17 percent had tried cocaine and 61 percent had tried at least one illegal drug by the time they reached high school graduation.[6]

There were 600,000 babies born to teenagers in 1986[7] out of approximately 1.2 million teen pregnancies.[8] What happened to the other 600,000 developing lives? Many were terminated through abortion. Others were miscarried, stillborn, or died later as a result of a variety of medical complications brought on because the bodies of these young teen mothers were not ready for the stress of pregnancy and childbirth.

Depression, suicide, alcohol, drugs, and teen pregnancy are not the only complex issues that can tragically sneak into your teenage life just as you prepare to make your final passage into adulthood. But these things are present in alarming proportions among you who are our future. Who you bond with and how healthy that bonding is can make a difference in your life. Having a special someone to talk to, cry and laugh with, depend on, trust, and love can be a much-needed buffer against the hardships many teens experience. This other person is often a friend of the same sex. Sometimes, however, it is a "steady" of the opposite sex.

Is it okay to go steady?

Dating one person exclusively in high school can be an excellent support to help you get through the many pressures of growing up. If the bond a teen couple shares is a healthy one—one that is born of mutual respect, enjoyment, and two-way communication—then this may be just the kind of relationship that will help see you safely through the latter years of adolescence. But, as I said before, you take certain risks when you go steady in high school.

For Liza and Jake, life appeared to be very good. They shared all their experiences and leaned on each other. They didn't really need anybody else. They didn't have to worry about having dates on weekends or making friends with other peers because they had each other. When Liza had problems at home, Jake would be her champion, and vice versa. They both felt that their parents were wrong and they were right.

They didn't pay much attention to their individual responsibilities toward teachers, local merchants, or upper-classmen because they were tunneling their sights onto each other and

If you concentrate on bonding
exclusively to one person in your
life . . . you may never learn how to
deal at a healthy level with your
friends of the same sex, your teachers,
members of your community, or your
siblings.

were only concerned with what the other one thought.

Do you see the risk here? If you concentrate on bonding exclusively to one person in your life, other relationships may be neglected or become nonexistent. You may never learn how to deal at a healthy level with your friends of the same sex, your teachers, or members of your community. You may not learn to solve problems with your parents or siblings.

Another risk teenagers are particularly vulnerable to is an "all or nothing" attitude. Quite often, teens think in terms of *forever*, *never*, or *always*. For example, maybe you've heard—or even said, "I'll love you forever, so why not have sex?!" Or, "I'll never get over the disappointment of not having a car to drive during my senior year!" Or, "I'll always hate you for grounding me over the holidays."

The risk here is that you may put yourself in the position of not accepting reality and you may fall into an irrevocable situation (physically, never spiritually). For instance, in reality a young teen couple probably won't be together *forever*, so bonding sexually is merely a form of expressing affection at best, a recreation in several cases, and even becomes a habit for some. Teens sometimes use sex to distract them from the normal trials of growing up—a way to avoid facing the hard issues. So, even though it is hard to abstain from sexual involvement, it is even harder to stop and tear apart a binding agreement once you start having sex. Bonds that show true love not only tie people together, they also set you free to grow and develop in healthy ways.

The chances that you'll *never* get over a disappointment or that you'll *always* hate someone who's stepped on your toes are somewhere between slim and none. Remember: *Time passes, things change, and you're stronger than you think!*

Proverbs 20:29 says, "The glory of young men is their strength." This goes for young women too! Not just physical stamina, but inner strength—the kind that is promised in Isaiah 40:31: "Those who hope in the Lord will renew their strength. They will soar on wings like eagles; they will run and not grow weary, they will walk and not be faint."

Talk about a sense of real freedom! You can take care that this freedom is not jeopardized by a carelessly-bonded relationship. You can count on your freedom and strength—no matter what terrible things may be troubling you—because God also promised us, "Never will I leave you; never will I forsake you" (Heb. 13:5).

What does this mean to you, a teenager trying your best to stand up under the pressures to make good grades, behave at home, look physically attractive, wear the "right" clothes, have the "right" friendships, and do all the "right" things at the "right" times? It means that there is one bond in your life already that can only be broken at *your* insistance. There is one love, one help, one strength, one freedom, and one source that is so right, so strong, so great and so perfect that He will *never* leave you—and that One is God!

The verse in Hebrews doesn't say, "If you have sex with your partner, I'm out of here!" It doesn't say, "If you steal, swear, take drugs, drive too fast, or stay out too late, I'm not going to hang out with you anymore." It means what it says: *God will never leave you!*

Regardless of how angry you get, how deeply you might hurt or disappoint Him, He is there waiting for you to ask Him for renewed strength.

One great thing that often happens when we realize the importance and permanence of this reality and accept the wonderful bond that God offers is that we tend to look at the other bonds in our lives from a different perspective. We may become a little more cautious about who we bond with and how we do so.

You may not be so quick to whisper, "I'll love you *forever*," in the back seat of a car. Or you might realize it is possible to get poor grades one semester without throwing up your arms and shouting, "Well! I'll *never* get into the college I want now!" It is even within your grasp to hold back when you want to rail at your parents, "You're *always* on my case!" In other words, a middle-ground is usually healthier for you.

What would be a healthy example of a teen couple relationship?

Cindy and Mitch went steady their junior and senior years of high school. They protected the bond they shared in order to keep it healthy and loving, without excluding or neglecting other relationships that help them to grow into well-adjusted adults.

When Cindy's 9th-grade sister, Amy, began to get serious with a boyfriend, Cindy took Amy aside in her bedroom to discuss the budding romance.

Cindy started cautiously. "Listen, Amy, I'm not trying to tell you how to live your life, or preach at you. I've just seen so many of my friends get too serious with guys too fast, think they were in love forever, and then fall apart when they broke up a few months later. I don't want to see you get hurt, Amy."

"Aw, Cindy," Amy shot back, "you're such a goody-goody! Don't give me that line about saving it for your wedding night—that's ancient history!"

"Amy, I didn't say anything about sex!" Cindy defended herself.

"Yeah, but I just cut to the end of the conversation! It always comes down to sex in the end, doesn't it? I saved you a whole bunch of in-between, that's all."

"Oh, Amy," Cindy felt a deep fear for her sister, and sympathy too. "I wasn't going to lecture you about sex. Sex is only one choice out of many in a real relationship!"

"Oh?" Amy seemed genuinely surprised. She added cautiously, "I'm listening."

"Well," Cindy hesitated, not wanting to close the small opening that Amy was giving her, "I was thinking more about the the emotional bond and how it affects your life overall."

Amy looked off into space for a few seconds, seemingly deep in thought. Then she looked Cindy in the eyes and said, "All right. You tell me how it is for you and Mitch. But promise not to tell me how you think it should be for me. Just give me your circumstances and I'll decide for myself from there."

"That sounds fair," Cindy nodded. "Let's see, how should I start? Mmm, I know. When Mitch and I first started dating we knew we really had something special. We were attracted to each other physically, but there was a lot more too. We felt so good when we were together. Safe and comfortable. After a few months we began to see that we had a lot in common all the way around. We liked the same kinds of music, movies, books, ideas, and people. We both wanted to go to college. We both had similar beliefs about God, family, and setting goals."

"C'mon, Cindy, all teenagers like the same movies, music, and that junk. That's generation stuff, not the material love is made of." Amy sounded cynical.

Cindy looked a little hurt, "Not necessarily, Amy. Mitch and I and our group of friends don't like a lot of things that go on in some of the other groups around school! Besides, that's my whole point—bonding with someone has to do with lots of things besides physical attraction. Tastes in things like music, recreation, and friends are important, Amy."

"So, if I like rock 'n' roll and my guy likes country music we're not gonna make it?"

"I didn't say that, Amy. You're really making this difficult for me! I mean that having similar tastes in general is important. Then there's the moral beliefs and values. Mitch and I together chose not to become involved sexually. We know that we've got plans for the future and we didn't want to risk what we already had together by getting too physical."

"In other words, you're just friends," Amy said quickly.

"Well, we are," said Cindy, "and that's very important for any couple, adults or teenagers. But we're more than friends. We're just not physical lovers. That doesn't mean we don't love each other. Actually, we love each other very much. That's one reason why we don't want to force each other by risking a pregnancy or disease, or by ruining the respect we have for each other."

"Oh, brother!" Amy was nearly hostile. "I can't believe you, Cindy! Don't you have a passionate bone in your body?"

Cindy was shocked, "Of course I do! It's really hard not to make love, Amy. Sexual expression is a part of real love, but for us it's also something to keep especially for marriage because marriage is the commitment behind a lifetime bond with a partner."

"Nobody waits for marriage anymore, Cindy!" Amy looked at her sister with disbelief.

"That's not true, Amy! You're buying into the lines you hear in the locker room. I think a lot of teens fall into sex thinking 'everyone else is doing it,' and pretty soon most of them are because they thought they were the only ones who weren't! What a crock! Amy, you've got to make your own decisions. Nobody's gonna take over your problems once you're pregnant or have V.D. You're on your own then, no matter how many others are having sex!"

"Wait a minute! We're only talking about you and Mitch, remember?"

"Then stop picking at me and let me finish! Sex is just one part of a relationship, like I said in the beginning. Mitch and I choose not to go all the way and I think you should respect that!"

Amy held up her hand, "Okay, okay, I'm sorry. So you guys have a lot of the same interests, your friends do too, and it's hard not to have sex—what else?"

"You left out plans for the future. We have goals for ourselves. College, careers, families, and all. In order to keep our bond strong we talk *a lot* about our plans. We talk a lot—period. If a couple finds that their only real sharing and communication is when they're naked in the dark, then they're in for some real trouble. Mitch and I go with our group most often. We hang around other couples who share our same beliefs about holding on for our futures. We try not to tempt ourselves to the point of no return with sex, drugs, alcohol, or whatever. We go skating, bowling, and golfing. We take turns having the crowd over to watch movies on the VCR—but you know that already."

"Why all the group activity?" Amy asked. "Just to keep you out of bed?"

Cindy looked for sarcasm in Amy's expression but found none. "No," she said. "We stay in a group to keep the bonds with our friends growing and strong. Mitch and I know that the odds say we probably won't be together for a lifetime, so we feel it's important not to shut other people out of our lives."

Amy looked like she was genuinely trying to understand. "So you and Mitch hang out with a group that has similar beliefs, tastes, and goals as you. And you say that helps keep all of you straight?"

"Right." Cindy was relieved to see that Amy was beginning to understand some of what she was saying. "And it also helps us to deal with our problems, too. If somebody's having trouble at home or being hassled at school, we can all talk about it and work on solving our troubles together. Lots of times someone will have an idea no one else thought of. And it might be all that one of us needs to put frustrating problems into perspective and work them out. Of course, Mitch and I talk alone about different situations, too."

"Sounds to me like you have a kind of superiority club going, Cindy." Amy's guard came back up and she was just as bristly as ever.

Cindy was losing her patience. "Listen, Amy, I don't know what bug's biting you, but we're all just teenagers trying to make it through together. We have some really special relationships and a lot of good things going. We try to stay out of trouble and help each other along the way. What's so wrong with that, Amy?!"

Amy's face turned ashen and her eyes quickly filled with tears. Before Cindy could say anything, Amy burst out, "Oh,

Cindy! I'm sorry! I wasn't trying to hurt you! I'm such a snot! It's just that—I—uh—I—" Amy gulped loudly, "I'm not a virgin anymore, Cindy!"

What is re-virginity?

Amy confessed her own traumatic story about falling into a sexual relationship with her boyfriend. She was enveloped in pain, grief, and self-hatred. Cindy wrapped her arms around Amy and held her as the younger girl rocked back and forth and poured out her heart. Another precious bond—that of family—was called upon.

When Amy's heaving sobs had slowed to periodic hiccups, Cindy gently pushed Amy away from her and looked at her with deep sorrow. "You can't physically turn back what's happened, Amy. I'm so sorry about that. But you can *inside* yourself!"

"What are you talking about" Amy looked at Cindy with swollen eyes.

"I mean spiritually and emotionally you can become a virgin again! Basically, what's happened is that you forgot the most important bond in your life—your bond with God—and made a new one with your boyfriend. But you *know* that God still loves you!"

"God?!" Amy looked incredulous. "What does God have to do with this? I tell you I've lost my virginity and you talk to me about God?!"

Cindy tightened her grip on her young sister's shoulders, "Amy, listen up! Why do you feel so rotten about losing your virginity? Because the sex wasn't good? Or maybe because Mom or Dad would get angry if they knew? But they don't know, Amy, so why do you feel so bad?!"

"Uh," Amy was abruptly at a loss, "I guess I don't know."

"God, Amy, God! You know deep inside you that you've hurt *Him*. That's why you feel so awful. You feel you've lost something precious that He gave you and you feel terrible about it! Remember when I was goofing around in the bathroom with that antique necklace Grandma gave Mom, and it slipped out of my hand and fell down the bathtub drain? I felt so rotten, Amy! I knew I hurt Mom real bad—I *knew* I wasn't supposed to be messing with it in the first place, and to top it off, I lost it! That's kind of like what's going on inside you."

Amy's eyes glistened with new tears and she looked pleadingly at Cindy. "Yeah, I know you're right about why I feel bad. I just don't know what I can do now. I can't get back my virginity any more than you could replace the necklace! Cindy, what can I do?!"

"Well, when I finally went to Mom about the necklace—remember how I tried to hide it for weeks as though she'd never find out, just like you've been living with this—she was so hurt. She was disappointed and frustrated. She sat there and looked at me with such sad eyes. I thought she would *never* love me again. But after a while she told me that what was done was done and she could see I felt really bad about the whole thing so there was no use in punishing me. Then I crumpled into her arms like a baby and told her how much I loved her and could she ever forgive me? She cried too and said that she did forgive me and that she loved me too.

"God's bond with you is even stronger than that, Amy. It had to have been so hard for Mom to forgive me. She must've wanted to yell at me like crazy. But she didn't, and she's human. God's perfect, Amy. He's already got a handle on your situation. He knows *you're* hurting. Now it's all up to you."

"That's the point, Cindy!" Amy sighed hopelessly. "There's nothing I can do to change what I've done!"

"Oh, yes! There is!" Cindy jumped off the bed and grabbed a Bible from her desk. "Let me look up something."

Cindy thumbed through several pages until she came to one with its corner turned down. "Okay, Amy," she said, "here it is. Mom showed me this verse after I lost her necklace and couldn't get over feeling ashamed. Colossians 3:13 and 14 says, 'Bear with each other and forgive whatever grievances you may have against one another. Forgive as the Lord forgave you. And over all these virtues, put on love, which binds them all together in perfect unity.' See?"

"Not really," Amy said dismally.

"Amy, the Lord forgives you. He loves you just the way you are! Now you have to forgive yourself and love yourself so that your bond with the Lord can be perfect again!"

Amy looked at Cindy with hope rising in her eyes, "You're saying that even though I can't change in my body what I did, I can make things inside of me just like they were before?"

"Exactly!" Cindy said excitedly. "Look, Acts 3:19 says, 'Repent, then, and turn to God, so that your sins may be wiped out, that times of refreshing may come from the Lord.' Repent means to be sorry for what you did and then change how you've acted. Tell God you're sorry, Amy, ask Him to forgive you and He will wipe out what you've done—He won't even remember it anymore!"

"Really?!" Amy could not dare to believe this at first.

"Oh, yes, really!" Cindy grinned. "In Isaiah 43:25 God says, 'I am he who blots out . . . and remembers your sin no more.'" And not only that—if you make your bond with God right again, then your bonds with people will be better, too!"

Amy's face seemed to shine as hope returned to her with full, young exuberance, "All right! Thanks, Cindy! Thanks forever!" Amy hugged her sister gratefully. "Oh! I love you, Cindy! Thanks! I'm out of here!" Amy jumped off the bed. As she reached the doorway she looked back at Cindy and said humbly, "I have a special bond to fix up!"

Cindy wiped tears of thankfulness, mixed with a certain sadness, from her eyes. She knew that Amy would be all right.

Whether the bonds in your life are healthy or unhealthy is your choice to make. You decide with whom and how you will bond. You can insist on risking your future happiness by neglecting relationships that truly need attention—and that especially includes your relationship with God—or you can take the time and make the effort to nurture all your relationships.

How you relate to the opposite sex, peers, parents, teachers, authorities, acquaintances and God is completely up to you. No one can tell you how or force you to be a certain kind of person. Your bonds with others will be as you choose them to be—strengthening, loving and growing, or weakening, despairing and destructive. Taking responsibility for the bonding that goes on between you and the people you care about is a genuine sign of maturity and of love for yourself.

Are your life circumstances holding you back or setting you free?

Choose the response below each item that most clearly fits your situation and with how you feel.

1. "My rules and restrictions as a teen seem like a ________ to guide me into adulthood."
   a. cattle chute
   b. water slide
   c. wide open hallway
   d. rocky mountain path

2. "I am looking forward to the future ________________."
   a. excitedly, I can't wait to live life my way!
   b. with dread, I'm scared to death!
   c. happily because I know, even if I'm nervous at times, I'll be okay!
   d. hardly at all, because I'm too busy having fun now!

3. "I feel that my life is ________________________."
   a. a treasure chest full of priceless gifts.
   b. a Christmas package full of great surprises.

c. a box full of junk in the attic to sort through.
d. a swap meet where everything's a trade-off.

4. "Most of my friends right now are ______________________"
a. easy, fulfilling, and fun.
b. restricting, stale, and boring.
c. complicated, demanding, and frustrating.

5. "When I first think of a member of the opposite sex I feel "
a. a little threatened and intimidated.
b. excited and happy.
c. confused and puzzled.
d. somewhat hostile and disgusted.

6. "When I'm with my best or closest friends, I generally feel ____"

a. free and relaxed.
b. uptight and on guard.
c. glad to be with them.
d. that I wish I was somewhere else.

7. "When I spend time alone with my parents or guardians I usually feel ______________________________________."
a. happy—I love it when we can spend time together.
b. cautious—something's usually up when we find ourselves alone.
c. defensive—if they catch me by myself they almost always start a lecture or find something to criticize me about.
d. safe—my parents may not be perfect, but I feel secure when they're around.

8. "I think school is ____________________________________"
a. a prison to hold me because nobody knows what else to do with teenagers.

b. something I just have to get through until I can really live.
c. a part of my life that's on the way to the future.
d. a real growth experience, a great part of my life while I go through the last phase of my passage into adulthood.

9. "When I think about myself I think I am ______________"
a. okay; I'm an all right person.
b. pretty neat, I like myself.
c. gross! I'm such a loser sometimes.
d. hopeless. I doubt I'll ever be happy with myself!

10. "I believe other people think of me as ______________"
a. a super achiever.
b. a real rowdy.
c. a goodie-goodie.
d. an all-around kind of kid.

Tally Up!

Give yourself points as follows for each answer you chose. Then add up your total point score and see where you fit in the "Point Totals." Are you on a direct path toward "flying free," or are you being held down by something?

1. a-10 b-16 c-14 d-12
2. a-12 b-10 c-14 d-16
3. a-14 b-16 c-10 d-12
4. a-16 b-12 c-14 d-10
5. a-12 b-16 c-14 d-10
6. a-16 b-12 c-14 d-10
7. a-16 b-12 c-10 d-14
8. a-10 b-12 c-14 d-16
9. a-14 b-16 c-12 d-10
10. a-14 b-12 c-10 d-16

Point Totals:

140-160 You are definitely a free spirit! You appear to be full of a healthy love of life and what it has to offer. With the optimistic and adventurous attitude you seem to have, life is probably going to turn up some wonderful, exciting, and humorous experiences for you! ENJOY!

121-139 With this point total it is most likely that you are generally a well-adjusted and happy person. There may be some areas of your life right now that aren't going so hot—is it with friends, parents, or self? But this could just be a phase. Overall, you seem to view life with a sound, happy outlook. Are you maybe facing some extra challenges, and things don't look as promising as they usually do? If this is the case, grin and know it will pass. Everyone has ups and downs. Things just don't usually go all good or all bad. If, however, there is something in particular bothering you and has been for quite some time, you might want to ask someone you trust for advice.

100-120 You may be going through some kind of depression, a distressing problem, or coping with a pessimistic attitude. Do people often comment that you "have a chip on your shoulder," or that you are "too defensive"? Is something really nagging at you? You appear to be grounded by your life circumstances or relationships right now. It may be wise to ask someone you respect to go over this quiz and your answers with you to see if there's a key to help you get back into a forward mode. If you already know what's bothering you—maybe you just broke up with a partner or your parents are getting a divorce—you may still benefit from the advice of someone you look up to.

Attitudes toward life, both the pleasant and unpleasant parts, can help carry you into a happy, fulfilling adulthood. Or attitudes can drag you down like an anchor around your neck.

The most vital thing to remember is that *you* are in control of your attitude. How you react to trouble and tragedy is a choice *you*make. Some people seem to have everything anyone could ask for and are still miserable. On the other hand, some people appear to have nothing, yet are full of joy and peace. What's the difference? Most likely, their attitudes! And how do you get a good attitude? By letting the seed of trust in God get planted deeply in your heart so that it might put down strong roots and grow until it is a sturdy tree that is an umbrella over your whole life! "I tell you the truth, if you have faith as small as a mustard seed, you can say to this mountain, 'Move from here to there' and it will move. Nothing will be impossible for you" (Matt. 17:20).

One of the very most important bonds in your life is the one that you have at home with your family. Your home life may not be ideal. Maybe your parents are divorced or fight all the time. There may be alcoholism or drug abuse within your family. Regardless of whether you have a sound, loving bond with your parents or an unhealthy, bitter one, you will grow into an adult—faster than you think. If your home is a happy one, then keep a special place in your heart and your prayers for those who aren't so fortunate. If you live in a home that is very troubled, know that there is help for you. In the next pages, we'll look at some different aspects of how our bonds with our parents and siblings can affect how we feel.

CHAPTER THREE

Home—Prison or Safe House?

Nineteen-year-old Drew grew up with much tension and despair. His mother and father divorced when he was 10. His mother remarried when Drew was 12. She and Ken, her second husband, did not have a happy marriage. This wasn't a secret to Drew or his two younger sisters. In fact, the children were accustomed to hearing the couple argue bitterly.

Drew remembers: "A friend of mine, Nick, was spending the night a few months after Mom and Ken were married. Nick and I were sitting at the dinner table with the rest of my family when Mom started harping at Ken about something—she's always criticizing and complaining—and Ken just took it for several minutes. My stomach started feeling tight and Nick was picking at his food with a real uncomfortable look on his face. When Ken had taken all he was going to that night, he slammed his knife and fork to the table and told my mom to *shut up!* Nick practically jumped out of his chair. My younger

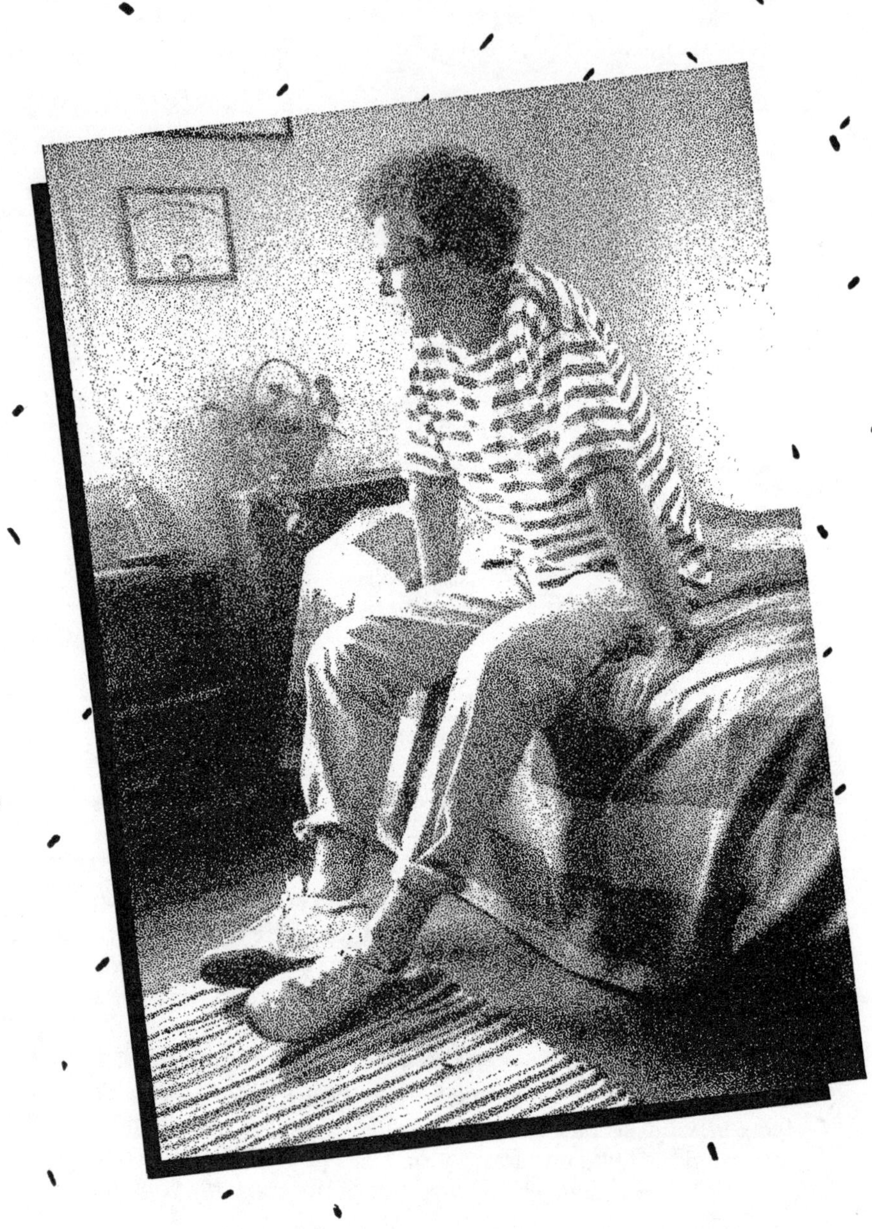

sisters started crying and my mom looked at Ken with this hatefulness in her eyes."

Drew gazes off into space and winces as if he were 12 years old again. When he speaks, it is with deep sadness. "Nick asked me later if my parents always treated each other that way. I told him they did—that was normal for our house. It's weird to be a kid in that kind of a home. You get used to the moods and tensions in some ways and in others you never do.

"The older us kids got, the more we noticed the rotten things that went on in our lives. Ken called my mom fat, lazy, boring, bitchy, and just about anything else you could think of. Mom acted disgusted at every little thing Ken would say or do—like he was less than a person. By the time I was 15, I couldn't take it anymore. I ran away and the police picked me up a few hours later trying to hitchhike. Things were really tough for all three of us kids then. Mom blamed Ken for my leaving, Ken blamed her, and they both started getting all over my sisters and me. Ken hit me a few times and then my mom would come screaming after him with a pan or something and beat him over the head! It was crazy! I would've gone to live with my dad except that he's taken off for who knows where after the divorce—I haven't seen or heard from him since I was 11."

Drew shakes his head as if to clear a fog from his mind as he continues. "I reacted to the pressures at home by staying away as much as I could. I started drinking and smoking dope with the guys and putting on a real rowdy-type attitude. Last year, though, everything changed. My next younger sister, DeAnn, was 16. She and the youngest, Stacy, who was 14, reacted to our home life by getting pretty wild, too. They were both in the habit of sneaking out their windows at night and cruising around until dawn with these guys who belonged to a local gang."

At this point Drew stops and clenches his fists in his lap. His voice is filled with emotion as he finishes his story. "One night I was hanging out around the front of this bar when DeAnn came running up the street. She was screeching like a hurt animal and crying for me to come help Stacy. I was half popped, but her panic sobered me up fast. She was babbling so that all I got was the part about Stacy needing help. We took off running back from where she'd come. A couple of blocks away I saw this pile of something lying in the gutter under a street light. It was Stacy. She'd been raped and beaten by one of the gang members while another one held a knife at DeAnn's throat and made her watch. Well, that was it. Everything just came crashing down around the three of us. Our lives were totally screwed up. We really had nowhere to turn for help that we trusted, but I knew if we kept going the way we were, one of us would probably end up dead. Actually, the pain and suffering we've gone through since the rape has seemed *worse* than death at times.

"That night, the three of us ended up at a hospital emergency room with a bunch of policemen. When Mom and Ken got there, I could hardly stand to look at them. I blamed every ounce of what was happening to us kids on them. When an officer asked Ken to sign a paper that released us to his custody, I broke down. I started yelling that he wasn't our dad and not fit to take responsibility for us! I said that it was because of him and Mom that all this had happened and that I wanted the police to put us kids in a foster home. It was horrible. In the end they made us go home with Mom and Ken, but a social worker came to see us a few days later. After lots of legal work, social service evaluations, and a judge's court order, we were all forced to go to family counseling. We've been going twice a week for nearly a year now. DeAnn is working on a major unhealthy attitude toward Ken—for some reason she's turned to him and they've gotten real close. Too close. She started flirting with him like she would a guy she wanted to date! The counselor says it's the only way DeAnn has learned to get a man's affection. I think it's gross! In fact, the whole situation makes me sick!

"I'm living with one of my mom's sisters and her family. I don't think I'll *ever* get married or have kids because, to be real honest, I think it's a bunch of bull!"

It doesn't take much in-depth examination to see that Drew's disturbed views of couple relationships and family life have been battered and scarred to a desperate degree. His parents' divorce, father's desertion, and his mother's and Ken's abuse of the privileges of marriage and parenthood have left Drew and his sisters depressed, confused, and hopeless.

The adults in these kids' lives reacted to their own inner pains, sicknesses, and suffering by outwardly venting anger at each other and toward their children.

Similar patterns of channeling emotional feelings of inadequacies, anxieties, pressures, hostilities, worries, and inabilities to cope with past hurts show up in a wide variety of ways in different family members and to different degrees. The effects of being physically and mentally abused as a child can crop up later in many areas. One thing is sure—such punishment acts like a constant drip of water on a rock, the kind that can wear down mountains or cut canyons through them.

Is there hope for kids from very troubled homes?

Dysfunctional families need lots of help, love, and care in order to balance themselves again. They *can* get better! Things *do* heal and your own personal ideas about couple relationships can become healthy! If you live in a violent or otherwise troubled home, *call* one of the phone numbers at the back of this book in the section, "Where to Get Help." Tell the counselor you reach what is going on in your family and he or she *will* help you get to someone who can help you right now!

If you're uncomfortable with the first number you call, then call another and another until you feel that you are getting answers to your questions that give you hope! I promise you that there *is* a better life out there for you if you will make the effort to find good people to help you on your way!

Not all families are in the dire situation that Drew's was. Some households are experiencing a temporary crisis or are distressed to a lesser extent. Your parents may be grouchy, sarcastic, critical, provocative, disappointed, or angry more often than not. Maybe you're not a direct target of abuse, but you live in misery all the same. It's possible that your parents cannot cope with your growing up, the turbulence of the teen years, and the dramatic changes that their own lives are going through. It may be that as long as their children were little and totally dependent on them, your parents could gloss over problems within themselves or in their marriage; but as the demands to interact more and more as a couple and as parents caught up with them, the fabric of your family began to fall apart.

It may seem that you struggle constantly to try and meet your parents' approval and are getting nowhere. Arguments, door slamming, pouting, crying, and feeling depressed may seem to be a way of life. Maybe you don't know how to meet everyone else's expectations or make life go more smoothly at home.

But take a minute to consider the situation honestly. Is your home life *really* troubled beyond control? Do you truly believe that your family has problems that are severe enough to warrant getting professional help? Be fair and be truthful. Keep in mind that *all normal, loving families have a wide variety of problems to cope with through the years!* Maybe your family seems to have an abnormal amount of pressure. Maybe reality in your family is too much for you to bear. If so, then there are places where you can go for help! Approach a counselor, pastor, teacher, doctor, relative, friend or older sibling. Or call one of the "Where to Get Help" telephone numbers at the back of this book. If you need help—GET IT! *You* must take the first step toward making yourself healthy and well-adjusted.

If your family is basically healthy and loving, but you feel as though you are under too much stress, try to analyze the probable reasons for it.

First, remember that during your teen years many things *seem* to go completely crazy. Your feelings can be terribly confusing.

It may seem, one afternoon, that your parents are disappointed with everything about you: Your hair's too long, your clothes are too tight, your grades are too low, your date is a slob, your friends are too wild, and you sleep too late Saturdays.

But the next morning you overhear your mom and dad telling visitors how proud they are of you, what a good student you are, and how much they love to watch you play basketball or see your artwork at the school show. They may speak of what great judgment you have when it comes to choosing friends and dates. You feel on top of the world.

The next day, however, you may again feel unloved, unwanted, depressed, and like you can't do anything right. "This is reality," you say. But by evening you're back to feeling strong, happy, self-fulfilled, and loved. So you think, "No, *this* is reality!"

Which is reality? Both—and neither.

These are the yo-yo experiences of life. They happen to everyone to some degree, but adolescents and teens seem to feel them more severely—for them, the ups and downs most people experience can be extremely intensified.

This is why one day you think everyone is against you and the next day everyone is for you. Your hormones surge and you feel like everyone expects too much from you. Your teachers, friends, dates, coaches, and especially your parents all want a piece of you, and there's not enough of you to go around. It can seem that you're not able to meet everyone's expectations, particularly at home.

Take a minute to be honest with yourself. Separate out what your parents *really* expect of you and what you *think* they expect of you. For instance, they may really expect you to keep your room neat, take out the garbage, talk on the phone for only 10 minutes at a time, be home by curfew, and speak respectfully to others. But to you it seems that they expect you to be an A-student, the best athlete on the team, the most polite kid on the block, the winner of the science fair project, to go with the cutest dates and run with the most popular crowd.

Go a little further in being honest with yourself. Remember we said earlier that two words teens use a lot are *everybody* and *nobody*. Things are rarely *everybody* or *nobody* situations. Think about it. *Everybody* is a lot of people! Not everybody can expect you to be perfect, hate you or think you're stupid all at the same time. Your parents may or may not have realistic expectations for you, but they aren't everybody, and it's highly unlikely that they expect you to be the best at everything all of the time.

The reverse is the commonly-heard complaint, "Nobody loves me, cares about me, listens to me, or approves of me!" Think about this one for a minute. Out of all the people in the world, it must be statistically impossible that absolutely *nobody* cares one whit whether you exist or not.

Everybody, nobody, and you. Sometimes that's how teens feel. All good, all bad, and no in-between. Sometimes that's how teens see things. You're not weird or strange to have these feelings. *You are not alone!*

Consider this possibility for a moment: Maybe it's not your teachers, friends, or parents who expects too much out of you. Maybe it's *you* who expect too much out of you! If you expect to have the only face in town without a pimple, the only home where there aren't any disagreements, the only physique without flaws, the only grade point average that never slips, or to be the only kid who never has relationship problems, then you are in for some extremely large disappointments!

People are people. We perspire, get ill, fall down, get scared, become angry, and hate. You are just like the rest of us. You will probably never be perfectly happy, completely healthy or have all the bucks you could spend. Give yourself a break. Go a little easy on yourself. Don't expect perfection from yourself or other people. A wise man said, "He who is faultness is lifeless" (John Heywood). When you are hurting, know that from suffering comes an opportunity for personal growth and strengthening.

Remember when you felt lousy and out of sync one day, and like the world was going your way the next? Time changes things, doesn't it? If your parents are on your case a lot or you live in an all-around unhappy home, you can hold onto the fact that time will pass, your situation will change, you will not always be a teenager, you will become an adult on your own, and you can make your reality more pleasant. Use this time in your life to quietly prepare yourself for creating a future healthy couple relationship and family life of your own.

Is there at least **one** *guaranteed source of help for every kind of problem?*

There is one, perfect, ultimate source of help for you in each and every area of your life—God. God is always available to you through the counsel of the Holy Spirit (read John 14:26 and 27), 24 hours a day, 7 days a week. It may be hard to hold onto this truth at times. Many teens have the same struggle with accepting God as they do with accepting life in general. He's real one day, and just a good story the next.

You may have a problem believing in God every day, but God has no problem believing in you. He said, "Don't be afraid, for I have ransomed you; I have called you by my name; you are mine. When you go through deep waters and great trouble, I will be with you. When you go through rivers of difficulty, you will not drown! When you walk through the fire of oppression, you will not be burned up—the flames will not consume you. For I am the Lord your God, your Savior" (Isa. 43:1-3, *TLB*).

If God loved and accepted us *only* for what we do or don't do—none of us would stay under His constantly available love and protection! As it is, 2 Timothy 1:9 says that God has saved and called us to a holy life, "Not because of anything we have done, but because of His own purpose and grace." We *cannot earn* our way to heaven! God loves us regardless of how rotten we are feeling, how mean or nasty we have behaved, or how miserable our lives are at home!

Some of the problems you may be having growing up are likely caused by guilt. You may actually begin to believe that you can't do anything right or that you are hopeless. Not so! Guilt can be an awful feeling—and a most destructive one! For example, Leslie cheated on a semester test at school. She got an undeserved *A* on the test, which was enough to pull her final grade up to a *B* on her report card. This *B* qualified Leslie for the honor roll that quarter. Her parents were very proud and said that she could invite two friends over for the weekend to celebrate the occasion.

Instead of being ecstatic as she would've been if she had earned the grades without cheating, Leslie was utterly miserable. She was filled with guilt. She was disappointed in herself, felt like an absolute fraud, and lived with self-hate for many weeks.

Guilt can be like a snowball rolling downhill—it picks up snow, dirt, rocks, and other debris in its path as it goes. Leslie became so full of guilt that she reacted by openly defying some of her rules at home. In this way she was "punished" for cheating by getting disciplined for being rebellious in other areas. Of course, her parents were completely bewildered. They could not figure out what had gotten into their normally well-behaved daughter.

The snowball rolled faster for Leslie. The more she rebelled and suffered the consequences, the more irritable and guilty she felt. One day she spouted off to her mother, cursing and stomping around the kitchen. Her mother walked over, grabbed Leslie by the shoulders, shook her, and demanded, "That's it, Leslie! I've had all I'm going to take out of you! *What* is eating at you?!"

Leslie stared back at her mother dumbly. Through all the weeks of misbehavior and inner turmoil she hadn't honestly been aware of why she'd been acting so out of character. She didn't realize that guilt was the culprit. But her inner self knew exactly what was bothering her. Before she even thought what she was doing, Leslie blurted, "Mom! I cheated on my test!"

Of course, Leslie's mother had no idea what Leslie was talking about. The report card and honor roll had been forgotten by now. After several minutes of sobs and confession, the pieces of the story fell together and Leslie's mother began to understand. She was extremely disappointed, but she could plainly see that Leslie had been punishing herself worse than any discipline her parents might hand out.

In the end, Leslie's mother convinced her that what was done was done, and that she could use the experience as a lesson that would keep her from being dishonest in the future. Although Mom suggested that Leslie tell her teacher what she had done, Leslie could never quite bring herself to do this. Her parents wisely accepted this and encouraged Leslie to settle the issue by asking God to forgive her and believe that He did, and then to forget the incident.

Romans 3:22-23 tells us clearly, "Righteousness from God comes through faith in Jesus Christ to all who believe . . . for all have sinned and fall short of the glory of God." And Hebrews 13:8 reminds us that no matter what is going on in our lives, the Lord sticks with us, "Jesus Christ is the same yesterday and today and forever."

God will never leave you alone or turn his back on you. In Romans 8:38-39 Paul declares: "Neither death nor life, neither angels nor demons, neither the present nor the future, nor any powers, neither height nor depth, nor anything else in all creation, will be able to separate us from the love of God that is in Christ Jesus our Lord."

These verses can be particularly comforting to teens during any turbulent times at home. When parents *seem* to think that you can't do anything right or you feel guilty about wrongs you've done; when you are full of anger, hatred, resentment, fear, and confusion; you can tell God that you are feeling these things and that you know He doesn't want you to harbor all of these emotions. Ask Him to forgive you for acting in an unloving way, and ask the Holy Spirit to guide you safely into actions of love, peace, joy, and faith.

How can I deal with anger at my parents or at God?

Brett's parents grounded him for getting home past his curfew. His driving privileges were taken away for the following weekend. This was extremely disturbing to Brett. He was 16 and had gotten his driver's license only a month before. He was dating Sandy, who was very special to him. Now he felt humiliated, trapped and powerless. He'd known on his way home what consequences he was risking. But he and Sandy had been having so much fun at the time that those risks seemed all right to take. However, now the consequences seemed out of proportion to the extra hour of fun.

Even though Brett's anger was mostly at himself for bringing on the unpleasant consequences of his actions, he lay on his bed and steamed aloud at his parents and God, "I hate Mom and Dad! They're so unfair! They don't care about me or how I feel! They like to punish me and see me squirm! And you, God, why didn't you protect me?! You know how much Sandy means to me—and you still let me be late and get caught! You didn't love me either! You're just like Mom and Dad and just want to see me punished!"

Brett was letting anger take over. He wasn't thinking like his usual self at all. Reality for Brett at the moment was anger and bitterness toward his parents, God, and—inside—himself.

Had one of his parents been standing outside his door and overheard Brett, he or she most likely would have been shocked and angry—nobody likes to be hated. Then Brett may have received further discipline for expressing his resentment.

As it was, Brett's 19-year-old sister, Diane, overheard his railings and stepped softly into his room. She looked at her brother and said, "Brett, calm down a minute. Want to talk about it?"

"Aw, what's the use?!" Brett snapped. "I'm grounded already! My whole week is screwed up and next weekend will probably finish Sandy and me! She won't want to date a guy whose parents treat him like such a baby! I hate Mom and Dad so much!"

Diane searched her memory quickly for an experience of hers that Brett could relate to his present circumstances. She winced as a painful memory from the past came back to her. "Brett, I know you're really mad. I don't want to preach at you and I do understand where you're coming from. But remember that time I told Mom and Dad I was staying overnight at Debbie's, and actually Lee, Debbie, her boyfriend and I stayed at the big hotel over on Sixth Street?"

"Well, yeah, but you messed up *big* time, Diane!" Brett declared. "You were 16—16!—and staying at a hotel with your boyfriend!"

"Brett!" Diane exclaimed. "You know the four of us were just hanging out by the pool and stuff—we weren't sleeping together!"

"Yeah!" Brett rolled his eyes upward. "But, you lied like crazy, spent a bunch of money, and stayed in a hotel with a guy—I don't care what you didn't do, it was still stupid! And you're gonna compare that to me getting home an hour late? Ha! Come off it, Diane!"

"Whoa, Brett!" Diane caution. "I just want to point out a few things I learned from that mistake and maybe give you a little different perspective on what you're going through. Notice I said mistake? Of course I screwed up! The whole situation was wrong! You already said the biggest thing—I lied. It took two years for Mom and Dad to regain their trust in me completely! That was the hardest part of the whole thing. Not to mention what Lee's parents thought of me, or Debbie's and her date's parents! I really blew it, Brett!"

"So, what's that got to do with me?" Brett sulked.

"Well," Diane answered, "what led up to that was a whole bunch of little episodes like you're going through today. Every time I'd break a rule, like curfew, or get into trouble for talking back, I'd go into my bedroom and get crazy mad, just like you. I'd holler and call Mom and Dad names and blame God for not helping me through. I let anger and resentment take over and never really worked it out of my system. I never went back later and told God that I was sorry, or explained to Mom and Dad that I knew it was my choice to break the rules and I was wrong. After several months I just worked myself into a roll. I talked myself into believing that any tiny amount of discipline that Mom and Dad exercised was a bunch of junk and *I* was the only one around home who knew anything worth knowing. I got real arrogant. I was mad most of the time. I think a lot of the anger was to cover up the guilt that was spreading through me. Bad feelings pile up, Brett, like moss on a tree. They can take over your whole way of thinking if you don't make things right and start over."

"Easy for you to say," Brett refused to give one inch. "You're 19 now and I'm the one who's grounded."

"I'm not finished, Brett. My lying and going to the hotel was my way of getting back at Mom and Dad for what I thought was their meanness. I was sure that every rule they made was to punish me, and I would break them just to prove that nobody could push me around. Instead of looking into reasons behind the rules—that they were to help keep me safe and healthy until I learned how to keep me safe and healthy on my own—I refused to grow up. You know that growing up means learning how to take responsibility for yourself, don't you, Brett?"

"Sure," Brett said, "but that doesn't have anything to do with being an hour late, Diane. You're making way too big a deal out of this—just like Mom and Dad!"

"No I'm not," Diane disagreed. "Look, Brett, you get home one hour late on a school night. Maybe you don't get your first period homework done, so then maybe you flunk a test. By now you're probably in a cranky mood, so let's say you mouth off to a teacher and get an hour detention. By the time you get home you're grounded another day by Mom for being late after school. Plus, you could've missed an appointment and messed up somebody else's schedule too. Almost every single thing we do affects someone else, Brett."

Diane continued before Brett could interrupt, "Now, you end up here, mad and blaming everyone else for your problems—everyone but you. You're the one who was late, broke the rule, didn't get your homework done, flunked the test, mouthed off, got detention, was late getting home again, and missed an appointment. Nobody else did those things. You were responsible, yet you're trying to give Mom and Dad and God the rap for them."

"Okay! Okay!" Brett shouted. "I screwed up! I did it all by myself! I can't help it if I'm mad!"

"Yes, you can, Brett!" Diane emphasized. "That's why I brought up the other story. If I had taken the time to stop my anger from growing and growing, I wouldn't have got to the point where I was lying and doing something so deliberately against Mom and Dad. If I had taken care of my rebellion each time I felt angry in a situation I wouldn't have let it build into one huge 'So, there! Take that!' toward Mom and Dad."

"Huh!" Brett shrugged. "It ended up being a 'So there'! to

you! And what would've happened if Mom and Dad's friends hadn't seen you and told? If you hadn't gotten caught, what would you've done?"

"Well," Diane paused for a moment, "I guess things would probably have gotten worse until I did something that really hurt me for life. As anger and resentment grow, a person gets more and more confused. I may have started to depend too much on Lee for love because I'd alienated myself at home, and maybe I would've ended up pregnant. I don't know, Brett. It's just that Mom and Dad really aren't that bad. You know they make mistakes, they're human, but they love us. They're trying to teach us to take these responsibilities one at a time so we'll know how to take them all at once when we're out on our own."

"I don't think letting me off this once would make me into a criminal, Diane!" Brett said.

"No, it probably wouldn't," Diane answered. "But how do you know they won't let you off? Maybe if you can get your anger out of your system and approach them sensibly with your feelings, they'll consider letting you at least go out one night with Sandy. Talk to them about a compromise. Tell them you'll do something extra to show them you want to work things out. If they still say no, then make the choice to say, 'Okay—this time I messed up, I'll pay the price with a mature attitude and know that Mom and Dad will respect me more forthe way I handle it.' Trust can grow between you and them, Brett, if you stay on top of your anger instead of letting it sit on top of you!"

"All right. All right," Brett said, "I get the picture. Take responsibility for my own actions. Keep a good roll going instead of a bad one."

"Right!" Dianne grinned. "Really it's just as easy to choose a constructive way to do things before you get overwhelmed by the destructive things. Teens get confused sometimes by all the emotional storms going on in their heads. But moms and dads get confused too. Here are these sweet, cute little kids they've taken care of and snuggled all their lives. To them it must seem that overnight their kids turn into moody, noisy people they hardly recognize."

Brett laughed, "Yeah, I guess it probably gets pretty frustrating. One week Mom and Dad are tucking us into bed and kissing us goodnight, and the next it seems like we're kissing our dates goodnight instead! Can you imagine having to make *that* mental change so quickly?"

"Really!" Diane heartily agreed. "I'll never forget Dad's face after I got busted for being at the hotel that night. For months, every time Lee came over here, Dad looked at him like a lion protecting his den!"

"Wouldn't you?" Brett challenged, "Geez, Diane, I still can't believe you'd do something like that! You're so together otherwise!"

"Sure," Diane nodded, "but it took something like that to wake me up to what was going on around me. Living at home is tough when you're a teenager. You're half grown up and half not. So half of you thinks you can handle anything that comes your way and the other half still needs Mom and Dad to make the rules! That's why it's so important to remember that *everything* we do can influence the rest of our lives. If we try to look at home as a safe shelter instead of an enemy camp, it helps keep us on a good roll while we learn how to handle both halves of ourself."

"I think all in all we're pretty lucky," Brett added. "Mom and Dad do love us and we have each other. Mom and Dad stick together on our rules and how they deal with us. Just look at what happened to Debbie. Things sure didn't work out for her, since the hotel fiasco, like they did for you!"

"No kidding! But look at what her home life was like. Her parents got divorced when she was 12. They fought all the time and put Debbie in the middle like she should be their counselor or something. Then they wondered why she was filled with resentment and depressed all the time. I know that, at least subconsciously, she got pregnant on purpose. Then getting married at 17! Now, two years later, she's in the middle of her own divorce. Who can be surprised? She really never had any good role models to teach her how to have a healthy couple relationship. She's just following in her parents' footsteps. Except she got off to an even worse start."

"Yeah," Brett said, "she's got some real big strikes against her. She's really got to dig in and let God help her learn how to put her life back together."

"Exactly," Diane responded, "sometimes we forget when bad things happen that God didn't make them that way. But He'll always help us start over."

Brett blushed, "I know. It was stupid of me to blame God for last night. He didn't twist my arm to make me late, and it's not really a punishment when Mom and Dad care enough to enforce the rules."

"Don't feel bad, Brett. We've all tried to put the load on God at times. His shoulders are wide, though. He understands and is patient. Now whenever my troubles are too big for me to handle, I give them over to God instead of blaming Him for them!"

"*Give* your problems to God, Diane? That sounds pretty squirrelly!"

"No, listen!" Diane said wisely. "Jesus says to come to Him when we are weary and burdened. He says He will give us rest—that He is gentle and humble and we can learn from Him. Jesus says His burden is easy! And I believe that. Just try it sometime. When you're feeling all torn up inside, tell Jesus you're tired and so you're giving Him your burdens so He can help you get your strength back and work them out!"

"That does follow along with what you said before," Brett said. "Taking care of things as they come along and not letting them pile up until you're overwhelmed."

"Right," Diane confirmed. "I think that's why rules and everything are built in steps. Nothing is good when it overwhelms. Too much of anything can be bad for us."

"Speaking of too much of anything, I'd better go look up

Mom and see if I can get out of at least part of my grounding!" Brett grinned. He went to his door and turned back to Diane, "Thanks for your advice!"

"Hey," Diane said as she stood up, "think of it as prevention for you having to go through what I did, and my way of helping Mom and Dad from going through it *again!*"

Brett found his mother, Judy, in the kitchen. "Hey, Mom!" he said. "How's it going?"

"Fine, thanks," Judy said cautiously. "What about you? I thought you'd be on your bed kicking and screaming about getting grounded."

"Yeah, well," Brett shuffled his weight from one side to the other, "I, uh, thought about it, but I'm trying to shake off the hard feelings. I know I screwed up and I have to pay the price. But I was sort of hoping we could maybe work a deal about it, though."

"Aha!" Judy looked at Brett closely. "I knew there was something going on! Have you and Diane been putting your heads together?"

Brett looked at Judy in surprise. But when he saw humor on her face, he thought he may have a chance. "Well, Diane did kinda help me work through my thoughts on the matter."

"I'm sure," Judy said. "What is it you came up with, Brett?"

"Nothing specific yet, but I will!" Brett was very encouraged by his mother's willingness to consider what he was thinking.

"You work on it, Brett. I won't say anything one way or another until I talk with your father, so don't get your hopes up too high. Rules are rules, and when they're broken, there has to be a consequence to help you keep on track for next time."

"I know," Brett acknowledged. "I just thought this once we could talk it over."

Judy laughed, "Brett! This is my second time around with you teenagers. 'Once' can lead to twice and pretty soon it's

Parents also struggle to cope with the demands of life and the consequences of their choices. They get confused and frustrated, too . . . . Just like teens, parents also need to know that they are loved.

every time. But I'll see what Dad says. That's as good as it gets."

"Okay," Brett said, and hoped.

In the end, Brett's parents stuck with the grounding. Brett wasn't happy about it, but he checked his anger and suffered through it. His parents were impressed with his show of maturity and they would remember it in the future.

Brett and Diane are extremely fortunate to have good role models in their Mom and Dad. Their family is intact and their parents have a happy marriage. God gives parents the responsibility to stand as a united front to guide their family and relationship. When a couple mutually lets God be the head of their relationship, and strives to keep their marriage strong and healthy, then the home is most likely a joyful, loving, and safe place to be.

Unfortunately, there are many divorces today and many unhappy marriages as well. Teens are having to struggle to deal with more and more confusion about healthy couple relationships and home life in general.

It is important to note that, as Brett and Diane touched on, parents also struggle to cope with the demands of life and the consequences of their choices. They get confused and frustrated too. Teens do not have an exclusive territory when it comes to disappointments and unhappiness. Just like teens, parents also need to know that they are loved.

Regardless of whether your parents are divorced or still married, trying to cope with substance abuse, physical limitations, or severe mental stress—they need to know that you care about them. And you need to know that you are cared about.

What is 'normal' in today's marriage and family life?

Choose the responses below which you think are the most

"normal" for today's marriage and family relationships. (Bear in mind that normal is whatever fits right in your family!)

1. If a teenager has a drug problem, do you think his/her parents would . . .
   a. kick him/her out of the house?
   b. get him/her to professional counseling?
   c. pretend it wasn't true?

2. If families had a choice, would Mom work outside the home or not?
   a. Yes, most mothers would choose to work outside the home.
   b. No, they would rather be at home with their families most of the time.

3. What do you think spouses like most about their partners?
   a. They are good-looking.
   b. They let each other know they love the other.
   c. They make "good money."

4. What do you think happens after most couples quarrel?
   a. They don't speak together for a while.
   b. They tell their friends about it.
   c. They leave home for a short time.

5. What percentage of fathers do you think express affection toward their children?
   a. 30 percent
   b. 50 percent
   c. 75 percent

6. What do you think today's families spend the most time doing together?
   a. Talking
   b. Playing at sports or games

c. Watching television
d. Eating out

7. What do you think is the most frequent activity a husband and wife do together?
   a. Watch television
   b. Talk
   c. Make love

8. How many mothers do you think openly express affection toward their children?
   a. 50 percent
   b. 25 percent
   c. 80 percent

9. What do you think are the two most common types of discipline for children in today's homes?
   a. Hollering and sending a child to his/her room
   b. Talking and suspending privileges
   c. Talking and spanking

10. Do you think it's better to be in a family today, or were people happier in the past?
    a. Today
    b. Past

Answers[1]

1. In one survey, 97.3 percent of the parents said that they would help their child get counseling.

2. Over 67 percent of the respondents said they would quit their jobs and stay home with their kids.

3. More than 61 percent said that they liked it best when their spouse let them know they loved them.

4. Nearly 70 percent said they don't speak for a while after a fight.

5. About 50 percent of the fathers openly express affection toward their kids by hugging, kissing, or patting them—75 percent show affection in some way.

6. About 60 percent of the families watch television together most often—30 percent spent most of their time together talking—25 percent eating out—and 20 percent at sports or games.

7. Some 66 percent of the couples said they watched television together most frequently and 50 percent said they talked when they were alone as a couple.

8. In this survey, 80 percent of the mothers openly expressed affection toward their kids.

9. About 56 percent said they talked to their children most often; 38 percent would also suspend privileges.

10. Although there is no "right" or "wrong" answer, many of the respondents said that they feel we are happier today even though our world seems to be a more dangerous place to live. One mother, for instance, applauded our ability today to face our problems and try to cope constructively with them.

Your family may or may not be like these answers suggest. It is vital that you remember that there is no exact right or wrong way to be as a family or an individual! If there is serious abuse, neglect, criminal activity, or other immoral behavior going on in your home, then go to someone you trust for advice, or call a "Help" number listed at the end of this book.

Otherwise, try to bear in mind that we're all human and we each have our own set of weaknesses, idiosyncrasies and faults that we struggle with. Try to let the "new" command that Jesus gave us in John 13:34 get deep down into your heart and grow there throughout your life: "Love one another. As I have loved you, so you must love one another."

What is real love? First Corinthians 13:1-13 gives us a very clear and beautiful description of real love. It begins with, "And now I will show you the most excellent way."

Regardless of whether your parents, friends or teachers get on your nerves, they are people just like you with hopes, dreams, and concerns. Try to accept their ways by loving them.

Friends can be a precious source of caring and support—no matter what age you are. We will discuss how to choose good ones and how to be a good one in the next chapter. The basic structure of a real friendship is the same with both sexes.

CHAPTER FOUR

Friends Are Human, Too!

How do you know someone is your true friend? Does a friend invite you to parties, share secrets, or pay your way into the movies? How do you act as a true friend? Do you feel sad for someone going through a bad time or happy for someone's victory? Do you stick up for someone who's in need of support? All of these probably apply in some way to your definition of friendship. Most of you likely think of things such as trust, respect, affection, and loyalty when you are trying to describe a true friend.

Friends also believe in each other. It is easy for people to say that they are friends, but to do things that prove this can be much harder. Friends care about and for one another. Jesus said an important thing about friends in John 15:13-17.

He said that we're his friends, and "you did not choose me, I chose you" (v.16). Notice that He used the word *choose*. Your parents are always your parents. Your siblings are always your siblings. You didn't get to choose them. But friends are *chosen*. In fact, even God *chose* us. It is our free will to choose Him! True friendships involve voluntary love, caring, acceptance, respect, and trust. Finding friends to share these vital things with can be much harder than you may think—especially during your teen years when competition in athletics, schools, peer groups, and boy-girl relationships can be so intense.

Do real friends hurt each other?

Sixteen-year-old Marsha has been recently hurt very deeply by Kate, who's been her best friend for several years. Marsha was attracted to Andy, a popular senior, for several weeks before working up the nerve to let him know she was interested in getting to know him better. She finally took an opportunity during a pep rally at school to sit with Kate directly behind Andy in the bleachers. She spoke to him as the students were getting ready to leave the gym afterward. Marsha asked Andy if he was going to the football game that evening and he said yes.

Marsha then swallowed her great anxiety over Andy's possible rejection and said, "That's great, Andy, if you're not going with anyone, I'd like to see you there."

"Sure, Marsha, I'd like that." Andy answered nervously. "Do you want to sit together?"

Marsha thought her legs had turned to rubber. She was flooded with relief and excitement. However, she accepted calmly, "That would work out fine. How about if we meet at the gate?"

"Okay," Andy said. Then they said good-bye and went their separate ways.

Marsha was so happy for herself that she didn't notice to cool glaze in Kate's eyes as they walked from the gym together.

It was lunchtime and the girls were walking to a fast-food restaurant nearby to eat. When they were safely a block or so away from the school, Marsha nearly exploded with joy, "Kate! Can you believe it?! After all these weeks I'm going to be with Andy tonight! Oh! I can't believe it—sitting with that hunk at a football game in front of everyone!" Marsha was moving along so quickly that Kate could hardly keep up.

"That's neat, Marsha." Kate said. "I'm really happy for you!" Kate's enthusiasm didn't quite reach her smile; but Marsha didn't notice. She was too busy bubbling over with excitement.

Kate was battling a wave of resentment and jealousy inside. She had also secretly wanted to date Andy for months. She hadn't even confided this to Marsha because she'd feared Marsha would laugh at her for thinking that a boy as popular and cute as Andy would go out with Kate.

Actually, Kate had no valid reason to think that she may not be "good enough" for Andy. She was a pretty girl, very sensitive, and normally pleasant. She was somewhat overweight and shy, and this ate away at her self-esteem. She didn't feel that she measured up to some of the slimmer, more outgoing girls. Kate was now irrationally hurt that her best friend would date Andy instead of her.

In reality Kate's anger and pain was at herself for not having told Marsha from the start about her attraction to Andy, but her outward reaction was toward Marsha. As they ate lunch, and for the rest of the day, Kate found every reason she could to distance herself from Marsha so that she wouldn't need to see Marsha's giddiness. Marsha was a little confused by Kate's seeming preoccupation with everything *but* Marsha's good fortune. After all, Marsha had been talking about Andy for weeks, and Kate knew how much it meant to her to go out with him. Kate knew better than anyone else how much nerve it had taken for Marsha to approach Andy.

What Marsha didn't realize was how devastating it was for Kate to know that Marsha had done what Kate couldn't work up the courage to do. Kate ended up staying home from the game that night. She couldn't stand the thought of being a tag-along and watching Marsha's beaming face next to Andy.

Saturday morning Marsha called Kate bright and early. She quickly breezed over a courtesy question about why Kate hadn't been at the game. She accepted, too easily for a so-called best friend, Kate's half-hearted excuse that she'd had a headache. Marsha then rushed headlong into a blow-by-blow account of her evening with Andy.

Kate's only relief came from the fact that she was on a private telephone in her room and could make faces at Marsha in her mirror as her friend described how "perfect" Andy was. Marsha rattled on for what seemed to Kate like hours. Kate made brief comments such as, "Oh?" "Yeah," and, "That's great" when they were appropriate. Otherwise, she wondered if it were really possible to have someone as a very best friend one morning and hate her 24 hours later.

Marsha was beginning to repeat the whole story for the second time when Kate interrupted abruptly, "I gotta go, Mom's calling me. See ya later."

Kate hung up the phone with a clunk. She looked at herself in the mirror, "Marsha, I'm going to get even with you!" she said.

Kate really had no justification for this vow of revenge. Marsha hadn't done one thing purposely *against* Kate. Marsha had done something *for* herself. Instead of facing the fact that she needed to resolve the painful issues within herself, Kate chose to blame Marsha for feeling so miserable.

It would have been much better for Kate if she'd sat herself down right then to think the situation through. She could have spoken to Marsha many months before her attraction to Andy, and things may have gone differently. Kate could have also spoken up about her feelings when Marsha said that she was attracted to Andy. She could have confessed her feelings to Marsha before or after the pep rally. Instead, she chose to remain silent and let her resentment and pain fester inside of her.

The next weeks brought more anguish for Kate because Marsha and Andy ended up hitting it off quite well. They saw a lot of each other. Kate's coolness toward Marsha made it easier for Marsha to turn to Andy and not feel bad about leaving Kate out of her life more and more. A friendship that had lasted nearly four years suddenly appeared to be swept into nonexistence.

Kate's anger and jealously burned as she watched Marsha and Andy laughing in the halls at school day after day, sharing lunch in the cafeteria, and driving away in Andy's car, smiling. Kate began spending most weekends at home alone, lying across her bed depressed. She became overwhelmed by her destructive feelings.

It is important to note that Marsha didn't have a chance to help Kate work through her feelings because Kate did not make them known to Marsha. True friends communicate freely back and forth most of the time. And real friends trust that they will not deliberately hurt one another. Openly confronting misunderstandings when you are aware that they exist is a vital part of being a good friend. Whether a breach comes becomes you are jealous, envious, competitive or insecure, you need to talk about it with your friend.

Kate's basic lack of self-esteem, coupled with isolating herself from other friends and activities in her long hours alone, contributed to her becoming extremely unstable, emotionally. She could have avoided this easily by sharing her feelings with someone—her parents, another respected adult, friends, Marsha, or a trusted sibling. It is important to understand at this point that your feelings are not necessarily wrong. Feelings and thoughts come and go, often without any encouragement from you. But when you allow your feelings and thoughts to express themselves in a negative, destructive way, then you can get really hurt. Feelings are not tangible. They simply exist. You *choose* how you will act on your feelings.

It can be very hard to reach out for help with negative feelings. You may be confused, ashamed and feel guilty about them. But it is worth the courage and effort to tell someone what's going on in your heart. You may be helped by someone's encouragement and sympathy, and by brainstorming solutions to your problems, or by simply accepting your situation. What you feel is real; you're *not* the only one who's gone through frightening emotions. Anger, resentment, and hate can be terrifying!

Ephesians 4:31 says, "Get rid of all bitterness, rage and anger, brawling and slander, along with every form of malice." To get rid of these things you most likely need to get them out in the open—the garbage won't take itself out of a house!

Kate didn't get her feelings out. Instead, she let herself be eaten up by anxiety, loneliness, insecurity, and hatred. Her hostility mushroomed.

Things weren't all roses for Marsha either. She and Andy had gotten a little too close too fast. Just a few months after they started dating, Marsha was pregnant! The only person she could think to turn to was her "best friend," Kate.

Marsha found Kate one day after school and grasped at a pretense of their old days together, "Oh, Kate! I've really missed you! I'm so upset! You've just got to help me!"

"Oh?" Kate looked innocent, but inside she was burning at Marsha's nerve. "What's the matter?"

"I want to tell you," Marsha started and then looked around to see if anyone was in earshot, "but not here. Can you come over to my house?"

"I'd like to, but I've got to get home and baby-sit for the kids while Mom does errands." Kate watched Marsha's face fall. "Do you want to come home with me?"

"Yeah," Marsha said eagerly.

The girls made small talk as they walked to Kate's house.

But once safely inside Kate's bedroom, Marsha told her story frantically, "Oh, Kate! I'm in such trouble! Last night Andy came over to get me to go to a movie. On the way there, he asked me if I'd heard the rumor that was going around us in school—that I'm pregnant! Kate, it's not a rumor—I *am* pregnant!"

Kate stared at Marsha in unbelief. Perfect Marsha? Pregnant? Kate smiled gleefully inside. This was just what Marsha deserved! Any sympathy Kate may have otherwise felt was swallowed up by a vision of Marsha and Andy in each other's arms. But aloud she said, "That's awful, Marsha! What are you going to do?!"

"I don't know!" Marsha gulped. "You've just got to help me, Kate! When I told Andy it was true he was so angry! He kept saying I had to get an abortion! I'm so confused!"

The panic on Marsha's face was so pitiful Kate grudgingly felt a little sympathy. On the other hand, it was a bit nice to see Marsha squirm for once.

"Well," Kate said, "if that's how Andy feels, it's probably best to get an abortion. I mean, if he's not behind your having the baby there's no sense in going through with it. And if your parents found out, they'd kill you!"

Marsha's pain burst forth in great sobs, "An abortion?! Oh, Kate, that's *horrible!* Kill a growing child? I can't, I just can't!"

"What else are you going to do?" Kate asked almost smugly.

"I don't know! Kate, can't you help me think of another way?"

"No," Kate said coolly, "I really can't think of anything else."

Marsha needed desperately to seek the advice of a mature, trustworthy adult. But she didn't. She gave in to her panic and the pressures from her "friends" Kate and Andy. She had an abortion at a free clinic in a city near where she lived.

Andy broke up with her. Kate twisted the knife more by telling some school chums about Marsha's abortion. The

Friends are human beings with faults
and weaknesses like anyone else . . . .
We must each take responsibility for
our happiness and try to leave room in
our heart to forgive others as we want
them to forgive us.

news was promptly spread throughout the school.

How can I forgive friends who've turned their backs on me?

Marsha learned the hard way that friends are human beings with faults and weaknesses like anyone else. It is healthy to expect and assume the best from others. But it is also wise to know that we all make mistakes and do hurtful things we don't necessarily mean to do.

We must each take responsibility for our happiness and try to leave room in our heart to forgive others as we want them to forgive us.

If you think about it, you can tell the different between a basically decent person who may hurt you out of their own insecurity, unawareness, or inner pain and someone who's just an all-around "bad apple."

Try to remember Matthew 10:16 where Jesus tells us to "be as shrewd as snakes and as innocent as doves." Don't set yourself up for heartbreak and failure, but don't go around hurting or tripping up other people either!

The passage into adulthood can be very painful at times. When you are disappointed by others, worried, depressed, or anxious, remember that you can *always* turn to God! First Peter 5:7 says, "Cast all your anxiety on him because he cares for you." No concern is too small or unimportant for God to help you come to terms with. All you have to do is give your problems to Him and ask for His loving strength.

Trust, respect, caring, and acceptance surface over and over again as the most important traits in choosing friends. Without expecting anyone to be perfect, you can make good, faithful friendships. Good times and bad blend together to make life richer. And we gain wisdom that helps in our passage into adulthood.

Is your attitude toward friends of both sexes healthy?

Read each situation below and then circle the number that corresponds with how you feel about how the person in the story handled himself/herself.

1 means you disagree with how the person acted
2 means you're not sure how you feel about it
3 means you agree with how the person acted

1. Astin found a wallet in the grass while she was walking home from school one day. In it was $50, a driver's license, and a small packet of what Astin believed was cocaine. She was shocked to see by the driver's license that the wallet belonged to her friend, Eric. Astin turned the wallet and its contents in to the police.

How do you feel about what Astin did? 1 2 3

2. Leslie discovered her boyfriend, Zach, kissing another girl in a dark hallway at school during a dance. Leslie turned around and went back to the dance without Zach or the girl seeing her. She didn't tell anyone what she'd seen. When Zach came to the gym, he told Leslie he'd been outside talking to some guys. Leslie acted as if nothing different had happened.

Would you have handled the situation this way? 1 2 3

3. Rob was very jealous of Tim because Tim got the position Rob wanted on their high school football team. To make matters worse, during practice Tim acted arrogantly about beating Rob out for the position. Rob waited until he was alone with Tim and then told him straight out, "Tim, you are really acting like a jerk. I have

to admit that I'm jealous that you got the spot I wanted on the team, but there's no reason for you to rub my face in it by bragging."

Do you think Rob handled this well? 1 2 3

4. Jason wanted to date Deb. She had just broken up with Jason's best friend, Tommy, and Tommy was really depressed about it. Deb had told Jason several weeks before she'd broken up with Tommy what she intended to do. Jason decided that before he asked Deb out he would talk to Tommy. Tommy was outraged. Tommy accused Jason of trying to get Deb to break up with him so that she'd go out with Jason. Jason could not get Tommy to listen to reason. The two boys parted ways on very unfriendly terms. Jason dated Deb.

Do you think Jason did the right thing? 1 2 3

5. Lori knew that Cara had a crush on Ben, but that Ben wasn't interested in dating Cara. Cara flirted with Ben, called him on the phone all the time, and told Lori how much she wanted to date him. Ben didn't have the heart to tell Cara he wasn't interested. Soon things got to the point where Cara was actually making a fool of herself trying to get Ben to ask her out. Cara simply thought that Ben was shy. Lori finally told Cara that she knew Ben wasn't interested. Cara was very hurt, humiliated, and angry. She blamed Lori for not telling her about Ben's true feelings sooner and said that Lori was not a good friend.

What do you think about how Lori handled this? 1 2 3

Discussion

Since there aren't always clear right and wrongs in our relationships, it is difficult to give black and white answers to how someone should cope with troubling situations. But there are usually healthier and unhealthier ways to handle problems. We all live and learn. Following are some points and questions to help you decide if you had a "healthy" response to each circumstance. You may want to use them to spark further discussion in youi class or group.

1. If you disagreed with how Astin handled finding the wallet, you showed a healthy sense of precaution. What if the packet in Eric's wallet was a prescribed medication or sugar substitute? Since Astin knew Eric, she could have easily asked him directly about the packet she thought was cocaine. If in fact it was the drug, she could have approached a school counselor in confidence and privacy to see what could be done to help Eric.
2. If you disagreed with how Leslie handled the situation with Zach, you're probably exhibiting a healthy respect for yourself and a strong desire to have a genuine, good couple relationship. Pretending that someone hasn't betrayed you will not make it go away. If confronting someone's betrayal causes you to lose your relationship with him/her, then the person wasn't really good for you anyway!
3. If you agreed with how Rob handled his situation with Tim, you are showing signs of maturity and strength! Rob went to Tim directly, yet not in front of others so that Tim's dignity may be threatened. Rob told Tim exactly how he felt, admitting his own jealousy. Tim could then choose to respect Rob's feelings or continue to act arrogantly. Rob faced Tim squarely but did not try to manipulate or bully him into acting the way Rob wanted him to.
4. If you agreed with what Jason did, you appear to have a healthy sense of reality. Jason told the truth, respecting his friendship with Tommy and having consideration

for it. But Jason did not buckle under Tommy's irrational reaction to Deb's breaking up with him. It was Tommy's choice to reject Jason. Jason apparently accepted that and dated Deb. It is important for all of us to accept that we can't always please everyone. If we do our best to be respectful and considerate, yet others choose to react negatively when we're not trying to deliberately hurt them, then that's their problem to deal with—not ours. We can't give up our own goals for fear someone else might not like us or will become angry.

5. If you're not sure that Lori handled things right, you're showing diplomacy and compassion toward human predicaments. Lori held off telling Cara about Ben's feelings—probably for good reasons. Ben should have dealt with the situation himself. They were his problems, not Lori's. Cara could've been more direct with Ben and asked him if he was interested in dating her. As it was, Lori was thrust into the middle of something through no fault of her own. She tried the best way she could at the time to help Cara. in Cara's eyes, that "help" was too late.

We all find ourselves in the middle of things we'd rather not be involved in sometimes. If we do the best we know how at the time, that has to be good enough. We learn as we grow and experience life. Ecclesiastes 9:11 says, "Time and chance happen to them all." An essential part of making the passage into adulthood is learning to deal with tough, sometimes unpleasant, situations.

The self-control and self-respect you gain from making choices about your sexuality carefully is tremendous. In fact, we will discuss sex, along with respect for self and for others, next. It is *impossible* to have a truly healthy couple relationship without self-respect, respect for your partner, and the respect *of* your partner.

How you act, speak, listen, and believe can help you to earn the trust and respect of your parents, peers, teachers, and others in your life. Having self-respect is essential for developing into a well-adjusted adult!

CHAPTER FIVE

Sex and Sexuality

Sex, sex, sex. That's all people seem to talk about anymore. Condoms, vaginal sex, anal sex, oral sex, AIDS, STDS, pregnancies, and abortions. I feel like someone cut a piece out of a whole sexual person and dissected it into little bits. It is so undignified—and *very* unromantic!

I mean, what value does plain sex have without attraction and magnetism? You know—he looks at you across a crowd, you look at him, your eyes lock, and something sparks deep inside. You know that feeling—where your breath seems to turn from regular air to helium and it's so light you feel wiggly in your stomach.

What's the sex act without all our senses being involved?

Squashing against a warm body in a sports car may have its moment of thrill, but it doesn't hold an ounce of weight compared to relaxing in the arms of a committed partner, anticipating the choreography of love.

When you have really blended your life with a partner and you trust that partner completely, sex becomes an exciting third act in a four-part play.

The first act involves the looking—eyes that glitter, nice buns in a tight pair of jeans, or a walk that you recognize a mile off. At this stage we often imprint on our minds forever the smell of our guy's cologne on his clothes or the perfume in her hair. This is when our hearts do skips and jumps when we see each other or stand close.

In the second act we touch. Warm skin, kisses, hugs, pressing together in a hungry dance of love. This is the prelude to two people becoming one. *Sex* has very little patience with the joys of this part. It wants to get on to the "real moves," never realizing that these are the moves! *Sexuality* says, "Yes! All right! This is thrilling and loving and wonderful and perfect!" *Sexuality* thrives on different levels of pleasure, while *sex* tries to take the steps three at a time.

The third act of sexuality is where soft whispers and wild play come together like a lazy river and rocky rapids—sometimes more of one than the other. Appreciating sexuality over just sexual intercourse can be the difference between a short, fast motorcycle jaunt and a long drive in the country with the convertible top down so that the wind rushes free through your hair and the sun warms your back.

The fourth act is letting your body and soul relax into a deep, soft cloud of timelessness. There is nothing that can compare to the slow, easy peace of snuggling into your covers with a loving partner you share your life with. Sometimes this stage is playful and laughing, and other times it's serious and dreamy. There are few moments as peaceful as drifting off into a mellow sleep or stretching happily to meet a new day after truly making *love*, not just getting it on.

Why take one quick dance when you can look forward to the band playing all night just for the two of you? It's the difference between wolfing down a burger from the drive-thru because you're already late getting somewhere, and leisurely feasting on a delicious, sensual meal at the best restaurant in town.

I think it's very sad that most teens are not fully informed about their sexuality. The Center for Population Options has found that over 80 percent of all parents never had a significant talk about sex with their kids.[1] And a survey of young people, who go to church regularly, revealed that 73 percent of them got little or no education about sex at their churches.[2] I find it terribly odd that parents fuss at their kids about whose turn it is to take out the garbage, that schoolteachers get lathered up over achievement test scores, and that church leaders worry over kids meeting requirements for confirmation, but no one is making sure you get proper guidelines and encouragement about your sexuality and couple relationships.

It's not that adults don't care. For the most part they do. But there's something about sexuality that is so personal, so delicate, and so special that it is very, very hard to discuss it with others—especially your own children, students, or charges. Something so special deserves respect—for ourselves and for each other.

One of the toughest aspects of learning to respect yourself can be your need to feel loved and to be accepted by your peers. Nobody likes to be criticized, ridiculed, or rejected. But teenagers may find these things especially tough to cope with. You may feel as though you're not pretty, thin, smart, rich, or athletic enough to have a "right" to turn down sexual advances. Maybe you're not part of the "popular" group at school and you feel that you are obligated to "pay off" a date at the end of an evening. In this chapter we will talk about developing a healthy respect for yourself, your sexuality, and your partner. But above all, remember that when it comes to your sexuality: *You don't owe anybody anything!!*

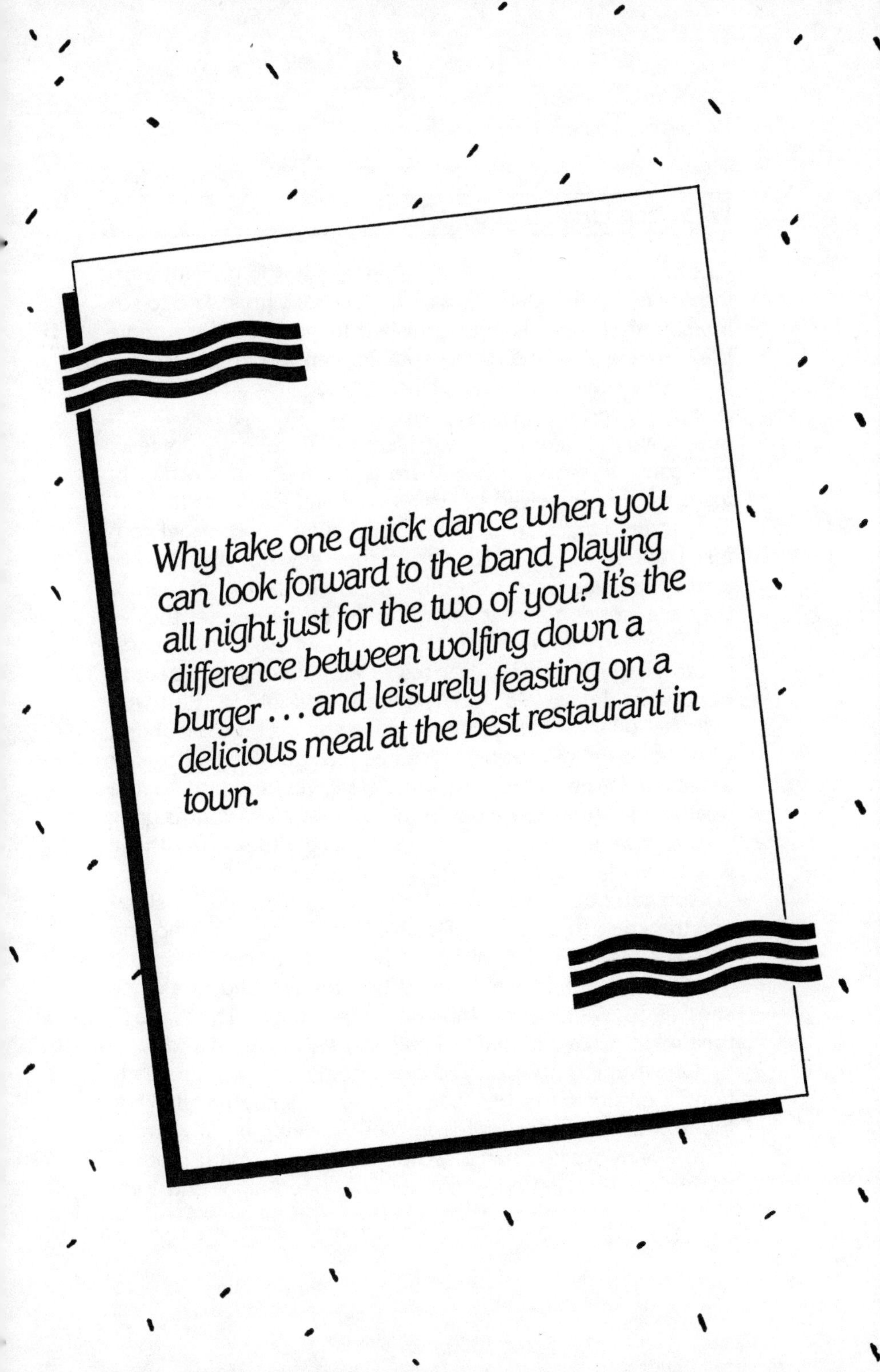
Why take one quick dance when you can look forward to the band playing all night just for the two of you? It's the difference between wolfing down a burger . . . and leisurely feasting on a delicious meal at the best restaurant in town.

What happens if I say no?

One of the biggest fears teens often face has to do with turning down sex on a date. It's as if the people who say no to sex imagine themselves being banished to some sort of remote island where all of the "unacceptable" people have to go.

On the other hand, most teens are acutely aware that they do not want to have to sleep around to be be accepted. This puts many nice teens in a real dilemma. To magnify the fears and conflicts even further, there is another large group of teens who are involved in sexual relations and want to stop. They want to experience "re-virginity," but are even more confused about what will happen if they say no after they've already said yes. They may think it's hopeless, that somehow they are condemned to sleeping around because they've already fallen into a sexual relationship. Whether you are trying to head off sexual advances or stop having sex, bear in mind what Jesus said: "Everything is possible for him who believes" (Mark 9:23). God knows that you get tired of fighting with the temptations and pressures that go along with your sexuality! Isaiah 40:29-31 says, "He gives strength to the weary and increases the power of the weak. Even youths grow tired and weary, and young men stumble and fall; but those who hope in the Lord will renew their strength."

You can become confident about saying no to *any* situation that makes you uncomfortable if you work on developing your self-respect and earning the respect of others!

Wendy, 18, had been baby-sitting for Ted and Sue since she was 14. Wendy thought highly of the couple. They were in their middle 30s and had two children who were 10 and 6.

One evening Sue and Ted came home several hours early from a dinner party because Ted wasn't feeling well. They found Wendy and her boyfriend, Mark, necking heavily on the sofa. Wendy was embarrassed beyond words. Mark made a hasty exit. Ted said an uncomfortable good-night and went upstairs to bed. Sue stood in the middle of the living room, wondering whether to take Wendy home and forget the incident or sit her down and discuss the situation.

She decided to approach the teen cautiously, "Why don't I fix us some hot chocolate, Wendy, and we'll have a little chat before I take you home. Your parents won't worry since we were going to be gone all evening anyway."

"Okay," Wendy said meekly. She felt very ashamed that Sue and Ted had caught them, and she feared they'd never respect her again.

As Sue got the hot chocolate ready she prayed that she would be understanding toward Wendy and that Wendy would trust her enough to open up in discussion. Sue looked upon Wendy with a sort of an older sister attitude and really cared about the teen deeply.

Sue brought their hot drinks and buttered toast into the living room. Wendy looked very small and young, curled up in a corner of the sofa, where, several minutes ago, she had been wrapped in her boyfriend's arms. Sue shivered to think how the course of Wendy's entire life could be changed by a few minutes of physical pleasure.

Wendy swallowed hard and her voice shook as she said quietly, "I'm sorry, Sue, I know I've broken your trust in me. I'm really sorry."

"Wendy," Sue said gently, "I'm not your mother and I don't have any authority to discuss sex or morals with you. But I feel that we've grown very close these last years and I think a lot of you. So I do want to talk about what happened this evening. I hope you'll feel you're able to do that."

"Sure, Sue," Wendy answered carefully, "but I really am sorry about all this. As far as sex goes, I know all about it. You don't have to worry about that."

"I don't want to preach at you, Wendy. I know that you understand the mechanics of sex. But just because you know how to have sexual intercourse and which birth control works doesn't necessarily mean you have a handle on your sexuality. There's a big difference, Wendy."

"I don't get what you mean, Sue," Wendy answered honestly.

"Let's start by clearing the air so we can be completely open with each other. If I were you, Wendy, I'd be sorry and embarrassed about being caught out with my boyfriend. But to be totally frank, I'd be more sorry I got *caught* than sorry for what I was *doing.* Is that the way it is for you?

Wendy looked back at Sue with wide-eyed admiration for a moment. Sue had gotten to the heart of what was going through Wendy's mind. But then doubt creeped into Wendy's thoughts. Sue *was* an adult after all. Maybe this was a trick of some kind to get Wendy's trust and then give her a big lecture. Wendy knew Sue and Ted were Christians. Maybe Sue was setting Wendy up for an old "fire and brimstone" sermon. Before Wendy could actually say anything, Sue did.

"Wendy, I can see by the expressions criss-crossing your face that I hit home. But now you're wondering how to react. Will I 'tell' on you? Can I be trusted? What do I know anyway? I've been there, Wendy. I promise you that not one word of what we say will be carried out of this room by me. I won't break any confidence that you place in me."

Can adults really be trusted to understand?

Wendy relaxed slightly. Sue and Ted had always treated her decently. She did respect them. And what reason could Sue possibly have to want to hurt her? A lot of questions about sex and dating had been running through Wendy's mind lately. She'd only gone out with Mark a few times. They were strongly attracted to each other, though, and the pressure was on to get sexually involved. Wendy would graduate from high school in several weeks and planned on entering college in the fall. Prior to dating Mark, she'd been able to exercise self-control—even though there had been times she'd stopped herself at the very last moment. She knew in her heart that if Sue and Ted had not come home early tonight she probably would have given her virginity away, and this really did frighten her now.

Sue was slowly sipping her hot chocolate and watching Wendy closely. She could see an emotional war battling itself out in Wendy's eyes. "What is it, Wendy?" she asked levelly.

Wendy hesitated, then blurted, "We didn't go all the way, Sue! I promise!"

"Wendy," Sue assured the teen, "I believe you! I wasn't accusing you of anything. I just feel like this may be a good time to sort through some of your thoughts and plans. You know, sexual involvement encompasses everything from the physical pleasure to your emotional health. A good beginning for any sexual relationship is when each partner has a large foundation of self-respect to build their whole relationship on."

"I knew it!" Wendy exclaimed. "This is going to be one of those 'God and your parents want you to wait until you're married' deals!"

"Wendy, self-respect has nothing to do technically with waiting or not waiting to have sex until you're married. Having self-respect means you are in a good position to make healthy choices for yourself in all areas of your life. I can't force you into a decision any more than God will force Himself on you, or your parents can make you do what they want you to. Respect, simply put, means to hold something in high esteem. If you think a lot of yourself then you have self-respect."

"What does self-respect have to do with Mark and me tonight?" Wendy was not totally convinced that Sue's intentions were going to be in Wendy's favor. It seemed to her that everything she and her peers did got knocked down by adults. All the scary lectures on teen pregnancy, STDS, and especially about AIDS, were getting pretty tough to swallow.

Wendy didn't want to get into yet another situation where she felt trapped and talked down to.

"Oh, Wendy," Sue said, "try to lighten up! I'm not out to get you. I have no reason in the world to be anything but honest and straightforward with you. As far as stuff like tonight, self-respect means you trust yourself enough to decide if necking is for you. It means you don't have to feel at the mercy of any pressure Mark might put on you to get more involved sexually than you want to be."

Wendy's eyes snapped with emotion, "Necking is *not* sexual involvement, Sue!"

"That's like saying that smoking marijuana doesn't lead to using other recreational drugs. It may not always, but there's a good chance that the more often you use it and hang out with the people who do, the more likely you are to eventually do cocaine or speed or whatever. The more often you neck with Mark while you two are alone together, the greater the odds are that you'll give in to your desires to have sex. A high level of self-respect can help you stay away from dangerous situations all the way around."

"Well," Wendy said, maintaining her defiant attitude, "what if I tell you that Mark doesn't put any pressure on me at all to have sex and that *I'm* the one who encourages a physical relationship?"

"You won't have very good luck with any attempts to shock me, Wendy." Sue looked at Wendy steadily. "I've been in your spot. I know exactly how you feel and what you're going through. I was the one in Ted's and my relationship who wanted to have sex before we were married. At the time I thought it would be the final seal of proof on our love. Fortunately, Ted had more respect for himself *and* me than I did when it came to living for the moment and paying the consequences later."

Wendy was the one who ended up being shocked. "You were the one who wanted to go for it and Ted wouldn't? Wow! Now I've heard everything!"

"Why?" Sue asked. "What makes you think any girl's sexual urges are any less than a guy's? Why do so many people automatically think that guys put all the pressure on? I do know that they have some of the more historic lines when it comes to trying to get a girl into bed. And often their physical needs can be more urgent and overwhelming. But, basically, males and females come together with the same momentum—God made us that way!"

"I don't know," said Wendy, relaxing some. "I guess all this sex and boyfriend stuff really does confuse me. I mean, when Mark and I are alone together, the physical part seems more important than anything else. Then the next day comes and I go to school, goof around with my girlfriends, and work at the deli. Life is right back to regular. But as soon as we're close to each other again, all I can think of is getting his arms around me."

Sue was careful not to come on too strong in answering. "That's perfectly normal. And it's also why so many adults try to encourage group dates. When there are other people around to interact with, your physical needs don't have nearly the chance to take control as when you're alone with a date."

"But you know, I've wondered—if I'm not alone with a guy, how can I get to know him well enough to know if he and I have a serious thing going?" Wendy asked, much more receptive now.

"It was my experience that things went in stages," Sue said. "If I went out on group dates with a boy, I could find out some basic things—like how much respect he had for himself, for me, the kids in our group, and other people in general. For instance, if a guy took pride in his own appearance, being clean and neat, then that was a hint as to how he thought about himself. I knew he cared enough to practice good hygiene. Then, if he was fairly conscientious about his grades, athletic performance, and not taking outrageous risks with his personal safety, I figured he probably had a good, basic self-respect. I could also find out how he treated other people. If he was courteous and considerate, I figured he had a normal amount of respect for his peers. I would cross off my list a guy that was a slob, didn't care about his grades or was always getting held out of team sports for disciplinary action. And if he was the kind who stood on railroad tracks with a train coming, or ridiculed peers in a group, or always insisted on having his way when we were making plans in the group, I could see a bottom-line lack of respect for himself and his friends."

"Um-hm." Wendy was listening intently. "I can go along with all of that."

"Of course, any guy who ridiculed the way I dressed, my beliefs, or my family didn't merit any of my time. I don't need people who don't help me to feel better about myself in my life! I don't think anyone does! We're all doing the best we can to get by in life.

"Another sure sign of lack of respect is the kid who is downright rude to his parents and other adults. There is a little rebellion or practical joking in nearly every healthy, normal teenager. But you're a smart girl, Wendy, and you know the difference between the guy who goes along with a harmless Halloween prank and the one who participates in something that's threatening and dangerous. A kid who's on the wrong side of respect for others is almost always short on self-respect too."

"Let's say you decided a guy in the group was okay respect-wise. What next?" Wendy asked.

"Then I usually concluded he deserved a little more of my attention. I'd scale down the group activities such as bowling or miniature golf to double date with another couple for dinner or the movies. As we did this over a period of time, I would pay more attention to how he interacted with people. Some sure signs of trouble are the guys who only care about what they happen to be saying at the moment, how they can talk you into drinking with them, or how fast their cars can pull away from signals."

Wendy's eyes lit up and she said excitedly, "What you're saying is that a boy had to *earn* your respect!"

"Exactly." Sue's wide, warm smile was one of happiness and relief—Wendy was a smart girl. "Just like with your parents, Wendy. As long as you live within the rules they set and treat them with consideration, you earn more and more of their respect. The number of rules you have to live by becomes less and less until your parents respect your judgment enough that they feel you can set your own limits. If you continue to live at home during college, your rules may be merely house rules that all of you abide by, just as you would if there were three girls sharing an apartment."

"Okay." Wendy got the point. "Then if a guy earned your respect and you liked him enough to want to get to know him on a one-to-one basis, like Mark and me, how did you handle that?"

"I made it a consistent thing to be 'alone' in public. I'd made sure our dates included dinners at restaurants, going to plays, dances, concerts, trips to the zoo, the beach, amusement parks, or any activity where we could interact one on one, but not end up someplace alone."

Wendy hung her head, "Like being together when you were baby-sitting for someone?"

"Just like that," Sue said gently. "We all want time together alone, Wendy. We all want to be loved completely by our partners. Part of a healthy love is having respect for ourselves and partners during our dating time—and that means planning your hours together carefully."

"But you said you wanted to make love with Ted before you were married!" Wendy cried.

"Yes, I did," Sue replied. "With Ted, my feelings went beyond dates together in public places and kissing goodnight on the doorstep. We fell head over heels in love. We knew we wanted to get married before we finished college. We began studying alone at Ted's apartment and going to drive-in movies. At first it was all right. We experienced the thrills of necking, but always had the self-control to stop before going all the way. We thought we were the 'good, Christian kids' who could handle ourselves. Until one evening when we found ourselves nearly naked on Ted's sofa and he put his foot down. He got up, took his clothes to his room and came back fully dressed. By that time I'd turned on the light and dressed myself. We had a long talk about the fact that, regardless of how good or how Christian we were, we were also very human."

"But you were in love, you knew you were going to get married!" Wendy quickly emphasized.

"Ah, yes," Sue said, "the ultimate excuse—'We're getting married anyway so why wait?' Ted and I sifted through several reasons for waiting. First, our Christian beliefs told us that we should wait, and that if we didn't we wouldn't only hurt ourselves, but God, too. And we knew that waiting to have sex until marriage would preserve the self-respect we'd worked so hard to develop. We figured the respect we had for each other would only be deepened because we were the only ones who knew how hard it was for us to wait for sex.

"Then, too, if we waited we would increase our trust in ourselves and each other to set goals and reach them—even when the going got tough. Also, we knew that our sexual relations would inevitably be sweeter if we came together for the first time when we got married. We decided to make sex a gift we exchanged on our wedding night—a present to each other that no money could ever buy and that we could reexchange over and over again.

"We also knew that until we actually married, something could change to stop or put it off—nobody knows what tomorrow may bring, Wendy. And we just trusted that our sexual encounters after marriage were ones that couldn't be duplicated outside the union. I can't think of any words to really describe the freedom we felt on our wedding night, Wendy. There's only one way to appreciate it, and that's to experience it!

"You know, Wendy, if you discipline yourself and train like crazy for a marathon, and then you bomb out when the day to race comes, you can always enter another marathon. But once you've had sex outside marriage, you can't physically take it back."

"I really do appreciate what you're telling me, Sue," Wendy said sincerely. "But what if I decide that I do want to have sex with Mark, even if we're not planning on getting married? I don't really know if I buy all the 'save it for one guy' stuff."

"Wendy, that also goes hand-in-hand with respect. If you are having sex just to have it, or as a way to show someone you really care about him, then it's actually a form of recreation. It becomes just like another dance in an evening and the specialness is taken away. Again, I have to say that once you've made love, there's no turning around. My personal opinion is that I respect myself enough not to let my body be a recreational vehicle like other toys people play with. There's also the risks that you take regarding unwanted pregnancy, disease, and other complications that come along with a teen not having a marriage partner to help her deal with them at a mutually concerned level."

Can you make things right if you've already had sex?

"What about the teens who do have a sexual relationship and then one of the partners wants to stop having sex and start that part of life over? You can't change the fact that you've had sex, so why wouldn't you just give up and sleep around as much as you wanted?"

"That's an excellent question," Sue acknowledged. "That very thing challenged my best friend. When she wanted to stop having sex with her boyfriend, we talked about it and made a plan together. She decided that her self-respect could only be complete if she could experience 're-virginity.' She knew that she couldn't change the fact that she'd physically had sex—actually with four different boyfriends that she thought she loved for keeps when she was going steady with them. But she also knew that she had every right to go to God, confess that she knew it was wrong for her to have had sex outside of marriage, and admit that she'd hurt Him deeply. So my friend asked God for forgiveness. She knew that He would literally forget her sins. You know, the Bible says that God will forgive us and remember our sins no more.

"Next, she had to forgive herself, and also forget. Then she had to tell her boyfriend her plan. And she memorized a Bible verse—2 Corinthians 5:17: 'If anyone is in Christ, he is a new creation; the old has gone, the new has come!' My friend respected herself enough to become a virgin again in her heart. She still had to live with the consequences of her actions because, when she met her future husband, she loved him enough to confide her past in him. Luckily, he was a loving, genuine man and understood her. He respected her courage and appreciated her great effort. But it could've gone much worse for her if her fiance couldn't accept her past. For her, though, it worked out. In God's eyes, and in her heart, she went to her marriage as a virgin.

"Later, my friend told me that only after her wedding night did she understand the difference between having physical sex and making love with someone. I admire her, Wendy. She's been married to her husband for 15 years now. They have three beautiful children. She's earned my respect in a way that no one ever has, because I know what it must have taken for her to retrace her steps and start all over again."

"Wow," Wendy was amazed, "that's so neat!"

"Uh-huh!" Sue agreed. "Hey—look at the clock! It's after midnight! I'd better get you home."

The two went out into the cool night, each with her own thoughts. As Wendy got out of the car a few minutes later, she turned to Sue and whispered a heartfelt, "Thanks."

Choices can be terrifically hard to make—especially those

that mean sacrificing a pleasure today for one in the future. Sexual choices are particularly challenging because they are made through faith in God's promise that "in all things God works for the good of those who love him" (Rom. 8:28). For teens, with all of life ahead of them in a vast expanse, it can be tremendously difficult to accept that it is better to wait to experience the good gift of sex.

Do you have a healthy respect for your own sexuality and the sexuality of others?

Read each behavior below, then circle the number that corresponds with how *you* feel about it. Do you think it's:

1—Unacceptable
2—Not sure
3—Acceptable

1. Discussing sexual feelings with friends **1 2 3**
2. Making remarks about what a great body someone of the opposite sex has **1 2 3**
3. Having sex with a partner when you know you really love him/her **1 2 3**
4. Having sex just for the fun of it **1 2 3**
5. Threatening to break up with a partner because he/she won't have sex to prove his/her love **1 2 3**
6. Discussing the pros and cons of waiting to have sex with your boy/girlfriend **1 2 3**
7. French-kissing **1 2 3**

8. Fondling your partner's genitals **1 2 3**

9. Being nude with your partner **1 2 3**

10. Enjoying the physical pleasures of how your body reacts to being close to a date without pursuing a sexual relationship **1 2 3**

11. Holding hands, putting your arms around each other or kissing **1 2 3**

12. Telling jokes about sex that are derogatory **1 2 3**

13. Spying on girls/boys as they shower or dress in the locker rooms **1 2 3**

14. Describing to your friends how a date kisses you **1 2 3**

15. Discussing sexuality with your parents **1 2 3**

16. Wanting to date someone just because you like the way he/she looks **1 2 3**

17. Watching X-rated movies **1 2 3**

18. Having a few beers or drinks with a date **1 2 3**

19. Living with a partner before you're married **1 2 3**

20. Losing control and forcing a partner to have sex when he/she said no **1 2 3**

Tally Up!

If you believe that numbers 5, 17, or 20 are acceptable, then read on carefully!

5. Threatening someone in order to get your own way is destructive manipulation. It does not show respect for the other person or even for yourself. A relationship that is based on threats is not healthy! Being a well-adjusted couple means making decisions together that affect you and your partner. You may not always agree on the way to do things. Then it becomes essential that you respect each other's desire to stay true to your individual values by accepting every person's right to his/her beliefs.
17. Watching X-rated movies or becoming involved in anything pornographic indicates a basic lack of respect for other people's sexuality, and usually of one's own as well. If people expose themselves to the dark side of sexuality often enough, they may become callous, perverted and so used to artificial stimulation that they can no longer enjoy a normal, healthy sexual relationship. Things such as orgies (wild parties where people often have sexual relations with multiple partners or in groups); bestiality (sexual relations between a human and an animal); or sadistic sexual practices (where gratification is gained by inflicting pain on each other) are not simply forms of entertainment! They are symptoms of a sick disregard for human sexuality. Some adult couples begin watching X-rated movies thinking that it will help improve their sexual relationship only to find that it destroys their ability to enjoy each other in a healthy way instead.
20. It is never all right to force your own selfish intentions on someone else! When a person forces another to have sex under any circumstances it is *rape*! There is no good reason for losing such complete control of yourself that you make someone participate in sexual relations when he/she doesn't want to. If you have forced someone to have sex with you or you have been forced to have sex, you need to seek professional

help immediately! Get to a counselor, pastor, or other trusted adult and tell what has happened. He/she will help you to understand your problems and then to solve them. Most often rape (date or otherwise) has little to do with sex. Rather, it usually has to do with some other deep, inner distress that is expressed violently through the act of rape.

If you feel that numbers 3, 4, 7, 8, 9, 12, 13, 14, 18, or 19 are acceptable, then please pay attention!

These behaviors are ones that modern society has largely portrayed as being acceptable. Actually, they often lead to trouble. In popular movies, books, songs, and in many adult circles it is considered harmless to make fun of other people's nudity or sexuality. It has become so commonplace for unmarried couples to live together, participate in sexual foreplay, and have sex as recreation that thousands of people think nothing of it. Many partners "tell" on each other's sexual experiences by joking about them and describing them in detail.

Basically, these things are all similar in a few ways:

1. They show a lack of respect for other people's sexuality.
2. They reveal a certain dullness about our sense of sexual joy.
3. They indicate that we have let self-indulgence become more important than the well-being of mankind as a whole in many ways.

A loving, healthy couple does not go around telling details of their sexual relationship. They do not betray their trust in each other by joking about the other's sexuality. They do not risk losing the special joy of their sex life by dulling their senses by depending on artificial stimulation, or by being concerned only with their own self-gratification.

A healthy couple keeps their sexual relationship private. They build each other up and share their joy as a unit—not in public. They work on problems and communicate disappointments to each other—not to friends or colleagues. A healthy couple demonstrates respect by appreciating their partner's uniqueness and God's gift of their sexuality.

If you feel that numbers 1, 2, 6, 10, 11, 15, 16 describe acceptable behavior, congratulations! Read on!

These behaviors are healthy and desirable. By using common sense and being true to your own values, you can be assured that you are showing a well-rounded respect for your own sexuality and that of others. Discussing sexual feelings with your friends, dating partner, teachers, and parents is a sound avenue of developing knowledge, understanding and self control. Sexuality is a good gift from God. Kissing, hugging or holding hands is a natural display of affection. Keeping this type of activity within safe boundaries that do not lead to sexual relations is a wonderful part of dating and getting in touch with your sexuality. There is nothing wrong with appreciating the physical characteristics of the opposite sex as long as you are careful not to ridicule or act maliciously toward another.

Respecting sexuality—yours and others'—is a basic part of maturing into a joyful, healthy adult. You needn't ever be ashamed of your sexuality. God wants you to enjoy it fully with a loving, happy marriage. Getting on the right track now is the best investment that you can make in your future sexual happiness!

> The pressures and influences of our friends and modern culture can make it extremely hard to make the right choices. Sometimes it seems so much easier just to go along with the crowd. However, we usually pay a price for doing this; somehow, somewhere, we have to deal with the directions we've chosen to take.

agers make a lot of wrong choices and many dumb mistakes. Wrong. Just the opposite! In the next chapter, you'll find examples of teens who are dealing maturely with sexuality.

CHAPTER SIX

Everybody *Isn't* Doin' It!

"Everybody else is, can or does!" This has become a classic way to respond when your parents won't let you do something you really want to do. Of course, in reality, *everyone* isn't, can't, or doesn't! But the pressures to keep up with your friends and the influences that affect what you think you want to do can be so strong that sometimes you may say, "What's the use? I'd rather give in to the pressures and influences than be a nerd!"

Sometimes it's better to be a nerd than to give in, though. Giving in can be very dangerous to your well-being right now as well as in the future. It's one thing to wear the same kinds of clothes your peers wear or talk the same lingo—these are usually safe ways to go along with the crowd. But giving in to having sex or doing drugs because others do can be the beginning of some extremely painful experiences. It's natural

for you to be curious about and want to try new things. That's the way people are. And they're especially curious about things that have to do with relationships, alcohol, drugs, and sex.

Nearly every generation that has had access to a dictionary has produced teenagers who went searching for words like *intercourse, vagina* and *penis.* But somehow a black-and-white definition in a book just isn't as exciting or revealing as most teens would like. People are more curious than that! So many teens want to know what it feels like to have sex, to be married, to be free of authorities, and to get high on cocaine.

Learning and knowledge are wonderful things. In fact, in Hosea 4:6 the Lord says, "My people are destroyed from lack of knowledge." Curiosity prompts knowledge and knowledge helps to develop wisdom. Wisdom is more precious than gold (read Prov. 16:16), and shows a healthy love of our own souls (read Prov. 19:8).

Knowing that curiousity is good if it is acted on properly, you should also know three basic rules to follow before you tear off toward unknown horizons to satisfy your curious nature:

1. Be sure the source you use to satisfy your curiosity is a sound, reliable one. Read good books, ask questions of people you trust and respect, and pray for guidance.

2. Before attempting to satisfy your curiosity, ask yourself: "Can what I'm doing hurt me or anyone else?" If the answer is yes, then back off and think your situation through!

3. Ask yourself, "Am I really prepared to get the true information on this, and can I handle the reality of the answers to my questions?" Sometimes we try to force issues that may be better left alone. For example:

Lori was curious about an affair she knew her father had had many years ago, a situation that nearly split up her parents. She prodded her mother to talk about it. This upset her mother greatly. Lori grew more curious and eventually asked her maternal grandmother about the circumstances. Grandma still nursed a bitter grudge against her son-in-law for the hurt she saw the family go through from her side of the fence. Grandma told Lori the "truth" from her perspective. Lori got much more information than she'd bargained for, and couldn't bring herself to speak with her parents about the issue again. She lived with a horrible feeling about it for years. Sometimes too much information can be harmful. Be sure that you're prepared for the answers you may get to your questions and remember that poor sources of information can be devastating.

Try to satisfy your curiosity reliably, safely, and realistically. Drugs and alcohol are big issues in the lives of today's teens. Curiosity about them and pressure to be involved can be extremely intense. If you are curious about the effects of drugs or alcohol you may want to talk with a group leader of your local chapter of Alcoholics Anonymous (see the Yellow Pages of your phone directory). Or you can ask to visit a rehabilitation program's center and ask one of the counselors about the realities of drug and alcohol use.

Tom asked his mother, Marge, one evening, "What am I supposed to think about older kids and adults I trust who drink and have fun? They're good people. They're not dead or paralyzed or in trouble. They're mostly successful, decent people and I don't understand what the big deal is! I hear people give testimonies about getting off booze and drugs, but I'm still curious about what it's like. If so many people do it, have fun, and get by without being hurt, how can it be all bad? Jesus even made wine for the wedding at Cana! I looked it up in John 2:1-11. I don't get it, Mom! Lots of honor roll students, athletes, and other people I respect drink sometimes. A lot of kids party their way through college and say they're the best years of their lives—how can I just ignore that? The pressure's really on, Mom!"

"That's a tough one, Tom," Marge said. "Your dad and I have just decided that we don't need to take the risk of abusing or becoming addicted to alcohol and drugs. We don't need to dull our senses or escape reality—we like our reality! And we don't use illegal drugs because they *are* illegal and they *can* cause permanent damage to our bodies and minds. We don't sexually abuse ourselves for similar reasons. Anyway, you get the point. At your age it's illegal to drink alcohol. Period. Also, you may *not* be lucky enough to escape an accident or death! There are always risks.

"If you want to avoid other people's ridicule for not drinking, Tom, you might make sure that you are a driver and say you have to stay sober for that. Or make it a point to have something to do early in the morning after a party, so you can say that you have to be clearheaded for this reason. Eventually you will gain enough self-confidence to say outright, 'I'm not drinking tonight.' Or, 'I don't drink.'

"Try to keep in mind that too much of anything is a form of roulette—you may be lucky, but you may not! We try to remind ourselves of 1 Corinthians 10:23 when we're making a decision in a gray area: 'Everything is permissible—but not everything is beneficial. Everything is permissible—but not everything is constructive.'"

Of course, one of the biggest areas of curiosity for teens is sexuality and dating relationships. Teens usually have all kinds of questions about their developing feelings and bodies and those of their opposite sex.

Heather is in a small group that a counselor, Mrs. Schuller, supervises after school. Teens in the group are free to ask anything regarding sex, dating partners, or whatever else they're curious about.

One day Heather asked Mrs. Schuller bluntly, "Basically, from all our discussions, you're saying that we shouldn't satisfy our curiosity about sex until after marriage, right?"

"That's right, Heather. It's more important to realize that satisfying curiosity often requires self-control and patience. You may be curious about many things that you can't or shouldn't run right out and do. You may want to know what it's like to be high on cocaine, but that curiosity had better be brought under control or you could find yourself in a whole bunch of trouble. Same with sex, driving drunk, talking back to your teachers or parents, and running naked in the streets! It's vital to learn that no matter where you go or what you do, pure self-indulgence can be a very destructive thing.

"Try to think through your choices. Ask yourself how others may be affected by your words or actions. Look outside of yourself long enough to consider that you are connected to a much larger network than just yourself. Think of a beautiful tapestry with lots of animals and flowers. If one ear is missing from a deer's head or one daisy is gone from the top of its stem, the tapestry cannot be complete. What you do affects all the people in your life's 'tapestry.' This connection isn't necessarily restrictive. In fact, it can be very liberating. Realizing that you have a special place in this world, and that there are people who need you and people you need, can free you to give help, receive help, and reach out to become the best person you can be!"

When it comes to controlling your curiosity, it may help to compare waiting for sex with looking forward to other highlights in your life. For instance, you thought you'd never make it to getting your driver's license, but you did. And you can also make it to high school graduation, on to college or your first job, and into marriage and your first time to have sexual intercourse! I know it can be difficult to wait for sex and to hold up under all kinds of pressures. But you *can* do it! Let's look at how.

How can I use what I know to deal with pressures today?

Nathan is 17. He is a well-adjusted teen with a healthy amount of self-respect. Nathan finds that when he is troubled, or is trying to make a serious decision, he is best able to deal with it alone, in the quiet times of his life. In fact, this is a sound guideline for anyone to follow. Isaiah 30:15 says, "In quietness and trust is your strength." Most of the time, Nathan trusts himself, with God's help, in the quietness of his own mind, to make his decisions and solve his problems.

Presently, Nathan is considering his relationship with Rhonda, who is the same age. The teens have followed the normal course of any healthy couple:

1. They met each other.
2. They were attracted to each other.
3. They got to know each other by talking, listening, observing, and sharing experiences.
4. They each liked what they found in the other.
5. They made a conscious, mutual decision to keep their couple relationship exclusive and not date others.
6. They trusted, respected, and cared about each other enough to share deeper feelings, ideas, and dreams.
7. They are now passing through a time of realization that their relationship is not perfect—there are troubles confronting them.

This is the point where the relationship is stalled. Nathan is seriously considering what they have going. In any relationship the outcome will be one of the following in order to complete the cycle:

8. The couple will consider their positions as individuals and as a couple, then discuss, compromise, and negotiate their way into a renewed commitment to their relationship. Or . . .

9. They will realize that they don't belong together, and one or both will agree to sever their relationship ties as they exist.

The troubles that have hit Nathan and Rhonda have to do with sex, love, and commitment for the future. Nathan is not prepared emotionally to commit himself to Rhonda totally, but he does want to enter into a sexual relationship. On the other hand, Rhonda wants to talk about marrying and spending the rest of their lives together, but she does not want to become sexually involved before marriage.

In his time alone, Nathan is thinking about his physical urges to have sex, and wondering why Rhonda doesn't want to share sex as a mutual expression of their love for each other. He is also trying to imagine how he would feel if he were to make a lifetime commitment to Rhonda. He feels real anxiety when he envisions himself as a married college student.

Rhonda, in her own time alone, is feeling confused, hurt, and rejected about Nathan's wanting to have sex but not willing to discuss a permanent future for them as a couple. She's finding it difficult to accept the fact that she may feel a deeper, more mature love for Nathan than he does for her.

Nathan and Rhonda's problem is common among teen couples. In fact, it reflects a common difference between many males and females: A male often thinks in objective, tangible terms, whereas a female typically struggles with the subjective, gray areas of the issue at hand.

For example, Tony assumes that Sandra will share his enthusiasm about going to a hockey game for her birthday. Sandra feels hurt that Tony would even think of such an insensitive gift for *her.*

Or, Cherie can't figure out why Rob doesn't want to wander through a jewelry section of the department store and daydream. Rob wonders how Cherie could choose to waste time looking at luxuries she knows she can't possibly afford. He wants to get to the men's section and buy the pair of jeans he went to the store for in the first place.

This is not to say that males don't dream about things they'd like to have in the future, or that females don't enjoy hockey! The illustrations are to point out that there are inherent differences in the way males and females view the same circumstances—simply because they are male and female, not because one way is right and the other wrong!

Figure 1 clearly illustrates how, in a healthy couple relationship, two equal halves can make the whole.

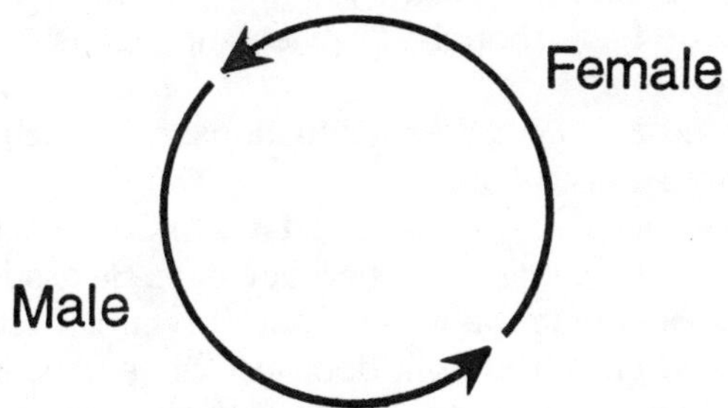

Though the halves are equal, they are not the same. If a circle is perfectly round, and set into motion, there is never one-half of it that is on the top or bottom (superior or inferior) position for very long. This is as it should be in a flourishing relationship—partners growing at their own pace, each needing the other to take the leadership in some situations; and able to trade places if needed in the next.

There are undeniable differences between males and females—they are equals, but *not* the same!

There are actually medical reasons for the differences in the two sexes. For one thing, due to a chemical, hormone-related interaction during pregnancy, boy babies will more likely spend their lives operating from the left side of their brains—the area of logical, factual and aggressive thought patterns. Girl babies, however, are more likely to start off using the right side of their brains—the source of feelings, communication, and creativity.[1]

From this biological fact you can see why it is vital for male and female to accept that, yes, they are equal—after all, both sides of the brain are needed and used. But, no, both sexes are not exactly the same. A man and a woman need each other to complete their circle.

To make life together as harmonious as possible, it is

important for men and women to take care in approaching each other. For example, women can talk facts to men as often as possible. Using logic in sharing with men will help put them more at ease. Men can try to be a little more communicative about their thoughts, while being sensitive to the female's feelings.

Following are two different situations; see which one you think is more constructive:

One day Meg decided she'd had it with Cory's habit of not calling before he came to get her for a date. He assumed that she would, of course, want to go out with him. That evening Cory showed up at the front door just as he usually did. By this time Meg had been stewing about the issue and was quite upset. She stormed at Cory, "You are so inconsiderate and rude! What makes you think I want to go out with you anyway?! Just don't come to get me anymore without calling first!"

Naturally Cory was completely shocked. Meg wasn't acting logically at all. He was put on the defensive and roared back, "What's the matter with you? We've been doing things this way for months! Why would I think to do things any differently now?!" He didn't look any deeper into Meg's obvious hurt.

—on the other hand—

Jesse and Lynn had been going out for several months also. When Jesse came to get Lynn he just pulled into the driveway and honked. Lynn's parents thought it was very ill-mannered. They asked Lynn to have Jesse at least come to the door to get her.

That night Jesse pulled in and honked. Lynn went on out. But during their date she said calmly, "You know, my parents would like you to come to the door instead of just honking for me."

"Why?" Jesse looked surprised. "Do they want to check me over everytime I take their 'little girl' out?"

"Actually," Lynn said, "I think it's more a courtesy—like the difference between a paper boy who tosses a newspaper at the door and one who heaves it into a flowerbed."

That was all it took—a logical picture that Jesse could relate to. He said, "I get it. I'm sorry I didn't think of it on my own before this."

Lynn felt good about Jesse's considerate response, and that they had been able to understand each other.

This difference in the way we think is carried over into the way males and females see sexual involvement. There can be conflict here just like in any other area. Let's look at the case of Nathan and Rhonda again, for example.

Fortunately, Nathan enjoys a loving, open relationship at home with his parents. His mother, JoAnn, is a very accepting and understanding woman and Nathan trusts her. Since he is coming up empty-handed about making any decisions on his own or with Rhonda regarding their relationship, Nathan wisely decides to consult with JoAnn and to lay things out in the open with her.

JoAnn is not surprised to hear of Nathan's concerns, or Rhonda's. She knows that the physical urges that push people toward sex can be very powerful. JoAnn has also watched Rhonda's and Nathan's relationship evolve, and has sensed that Rhonda has been moving toward a complete commitment much more rapidly and seriously than Nathan.

What is real love? How does it act?

JoAnn began talking with Nathan by asking him a timeless question: "Do you love Rhonda?"

"Aw, Mom," Nathan complained, "you sound like Rhonda! Yes, I love her, but evidently not in the way she wants me to."

"Bear with me, Nathan," JoAnn said. "I'm just wanting to see your first reactions to some basic questions. Without taking Rhonda's feelings into consideration, tell me *how* you love her."

Nathan's eyebrows raised in question, "What do you mean, *how* I love her?"

"I mean, are you in love, do you love her emotionally, or is it only a physical thing?" JoAnn quizzed.

Nathan responded, "I guess that's a hard question. My instincts say to answer with another question, 'What *is* real love?'"

"Ah," JoAnn sighed, "the mighty question of many ages. I can only give you my own definition, Nathan, but I think after being happily married for more than 20 years I am a fairly reliable source! First, I think it is essential to remember that words of love must be put into action before real, lasting love can be present. Many people say they love another and then use, manipulate, or disregard their partner. That's most often not love, but lust and self-indulgence. It just isn't possible to say that you love someone without acting lovingly. Loving actions can be so many things—making considerate phone calls, offering compliments, giving hugs, cooking a meal for a tired partner, saying you're proud of her, being on time for appointments and dates, keeping quiet when the other needs only to talk, sending a card of encouragement to someone who's struggling, sexually expressing love to your spouse, and wiping a hurting partner's tears when you'd rather be sleeping. Those can all say, 'I love you' much louder than words."

"Well, if you put it that way, I guess I love Rhonda and I don't—all at the same time. I do try to be considerate, I would like to be sexually involved, and I hug Rhonda when she cries. But I'm not ready to pick up the slack for her as I would need to do to be completely committed. I don't want to think of her or anyone else that way just yet. I want to concentrate on getting me into the good stuff of life. In other words, I don't want to be cooking dinner for someone else who's tired—I'm still at the stage where I want dinner cooked for me instead!"

"Very wise summing up, Nathan," JoAnn nodded. "What

you've just told me is that Rhonda is important in your life and you would like to take her to bed. But you do not want to make any promises to someone that you're not prepared to keep. That's very mature—it would've been easy to tell Rhonda what you knew she wanted to hear in order to get her into bed."

"Ha!" Nathan laughed. "It wouldn't have worked. Rhonda has a big thing about waiting for sex until she's married."

"And do you respect her for that?" JoAnn asked.

"I do, but I'm not all that happy about it. I mean, we *are* in love, and what's wrong with sharing that sexually?"

What if we have sex and find out later we're not still in love?

"Mmm, I believe I know what line of thought you're following, Nathan. So many people get involved sexually with a similar philosophy. Basically it says, 'What's a little sex between lovers?' Am I right?"

Nathan sat a little lower in his chair, "Yeah, I guess. But jeez, we *are* nearly 18 and we'll be going to college next year. We're almost adults."

"Yes, you are *almost* adults," JoAnn emphasized. "That's where many teens trip up. It seems that they think of themselves as miniature adults. But they're not. Miniature means the same, only smaller. Teens are *not* the same as adults! What is a pleasurable, loving, bonding expression between married adults can be an extreme burden for young people. A 'little' sex in a premature couple commitment can mean a lot of harm, Nathan."

"What kind of harm?!" Nathan demanded to know.

"The kind of harm that can eat up a relationship and the people involved. Let's say that you and Rhonda decide to go ahead and have a sexual relationship." JoAnn blushed slightly—it was one thing to talk about sex objectively, and another thing to bring it down to a very personal level with her son. But she felt deep inside that it was worth it for Nathan's future self-confidence and safety. "Things start to crop up. Rhonda could have nagging doubts about whether you would still love her if you hadn't become sexually involved. You might mistrust Rhonda—if she was willing to have sex with *you* outside of marriage, she just may be having sex with someone else, too. You might disrespect yourself for not having control of your body. And you both would be disappointed if you discovered that you were really only attracted to the physical aspect of the relationship. Also, there's the problem of possible pregnancy, or disease. And the kind of fear and false pride that blackmails a teen couple into staying together long after they may have otherwise broken up."

"Huh? What do you mean?"

"I guess I'm a little embarrassed talking right to you about your own sex life, but I'm going to be very blunt anyway, so hang in there with me, okay?"

Nathan nodded and JoAnn rushed on, "Okay, suppose you are sexually involved, but things start cooling off between you otherwise. You begin noticing other girls, you're fighting a lot with Rhonda and, overall, you'd really like to break up. But, you put it off because the two of you know that you began your sexual relationship with a sincere commitment to each other—maybe even promised each other you'd get married. Now, to break up seems a mockery of that commitment. You're afraid of being ridiculed if Rhonda tells others that you backed out on her. Being afraid of Rhonda's contempt because you chose not to go through with your end of the promises may prevent you from taking the initiative to go your own way. False pride may become larger than your common sense and you may find yourself saying, 'Okay—I said I loved her and we'd stay together always and that's the way it's going to be even it it kills me!' It could kill you, Nathan, emotionally. You could settle for a lukewarm romance while secretly hoping that Rhonda would take the initiative and call it quits on the relationship.

"But you are playing a dangerous kind of roulette with this type of attitude. Suppose one of you finally musters the confidence and courage to say, 'That's it—I quit! Even if I did promise to love you always, even if I did compromise my morals, and even if I have found out the hard way that I'm not ready to commit only to you—I'm still an all-right person who plainly made a mistake!' But suppose that by this time Rhonda discovers she's pregnant."

"All right! All right!" Nathan interrupted loudly. "Stop! Now that I've had sex just for fun and discovered that I'm feeling doubt, mistrust, disrespect, disappointment; and now that I'm afraid, full of false pride, have AIDS, and Rhonda's pregnant, what would you suggest I do with the part of me that still wants to go for it?"

JoAnn couldn't help but laugh, "I'd suggest you learn some self-control and stay busy with other things!"

Are movies, television, and even liberal adults right to encourage premarital sex?

"Easy for you to say!" Nathan quipped. "You don't care about staying in love. You don't have to deal with all the beautiful people in movies and magazines who are traveling abroad with drinks in their hands, smiles on their faces, and bodies that could make a hundred-year-old man drool!"

"Oh! Oh! Oh!" JoAnn cautioned. "Hold it right there! I'm not blind, Nathan. I see what the beautiful people look like on the screen and in photos! Everyone has times when he wishes he were a perfect piece of flesh, or was dating one. But we have to be mature enough to accept that what we see in the media is just the illusion of perfection—perfection doesn't exist! The cultural influence on our sexuality is outrageous. None of us is immune."

"Okay, so now we're sex-seeking zombies—victims of every media campaign—now what?"

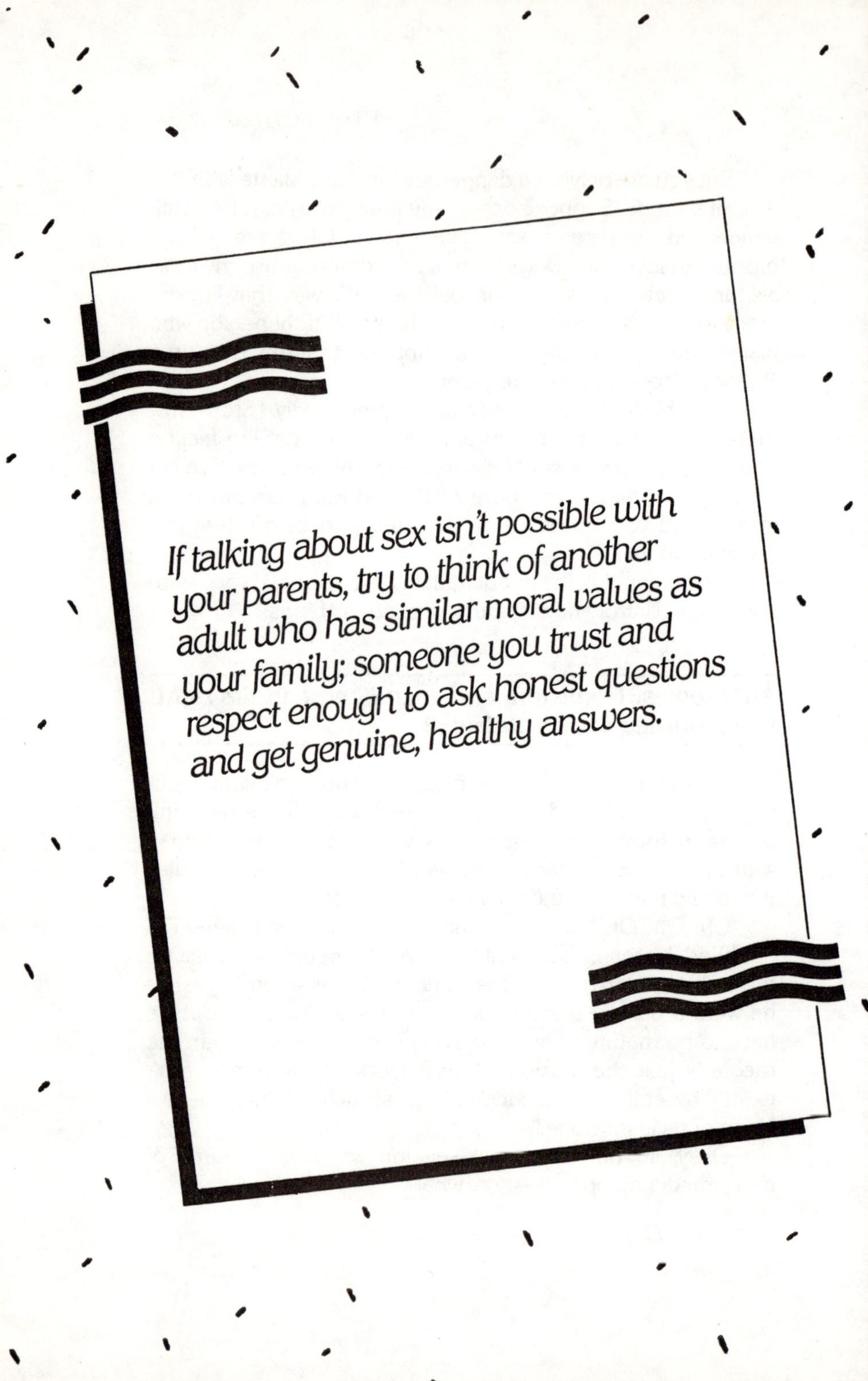
If talking about sex isn't possible with
your parents, try to think of another
adult who has similar moral values as
your family; someone you trust and
respect enough to ask honest questions
and get genuine, healthy answers.

"Now we need to examine to what extent we're affected. We can think about what clothes we buy, what make-up we wear, what cars we drive, and then ask ourselves why. We may need to risk the disapproval of others to keep sexuality in its proper perspective. I mean, do you think the right kind of jeans or soda is going to win you the sex bomb of the year award? And if they did, would you want that kind of trophy?"

Nathan smiled playfully, "Maybe."

"Hmpf!" JoAnn exclaimed. "Remember this, Nathan: We all have times when we'd like to recapture the sexual attraction and excitement of being in love, but life does go on and we also need to work on keeping a healthy balance of excitement and real living. You don't see Dad and me going out on each other just to be excited for a few nights, do you?"

It was Nathan's turn to blush, "Mom! Don't say that! I don't want to hear about your sex life!"

"You don't have to, Nathan. That's a private subject between Dad and me. And it will be between you and your wife someday. For now you can live and love without having sex. I understand that the final choice about what you do is yours—it's between you and God and Rhonda. But I also trust you to make the right decision, Nathan, because you have a good head on your shoulders and you know how to sift through what's good or bad for you!"

"Thanks, Mom." Nathan beamed and then grew somber. "I wish I had that same confidence in me!"

"You do, Nathan, you just have to call on it!"

Many teens are not as fortunate as Nathan. Many do not have parents who are able to discuss sexuality and couple relationships with their children as easily as JoAnn did. Try to remember that parents are human beings with weaknesses just like anyone else. If talking about sex isn't possible with your parents, try to think of another adult who has similar moral values as your family; someone you trust and respect enough to ask honest questions and get genuine, healthy answers.

Do the influences of peers and society prompt you to take more risks than you probably should?

Choose the response that fits your personality style the closest in the following situations:

1. If you're going to change your hairstyle dramatically, pierce your ears several times in each ear, or stay unexpectedly at school after a football game for a dance, would you . . .
   a. ask your parents' permission first?
   b. tell your parents what you were planning, but do it regardless of whether they approved or not?
   c. show them *after* you did it?
   d. choose none of the above. I wouldn't radically change my style or plans on the spur of the moment.

2. *If* you decided to have sex with a partner, which of the following would you most likely do about birth control?
   a. Nothing—only "bad" kids *plan* for sex by getting birth control.
   b. Go to the doctor/pharmacy and get the best kind for me.
   c. Ask a friend to buy it for me.
   d. Nothing—that's my partner's responsibility.

3. Which of the following would you most easily do?
   a. Drink a couple of beers at a party.
   b. Smoke pot with a trusted friend.
   c. Drive faster than the speed limit.
   d. Hike all by yourself into a wilderness area where you'd never been before.
   e. None of the above.

4. If you suddenly had all the money you wanted in the world, which of the following would you do/buy first?
   a. Open up a savings account—get that interest coming in!

b. Arrange to have a swimming pool put in the backyard.
c. Buy an expensive sports car.
d. Plan a trip around the world.

5. Are most of your friends . . .
   a. outgoing and adventureous?
   b. shy and reserved?
   c. intellectuals?
   d. rebels?

6. Are your friends . . .
   a. a lot like you?
   b. opposite of you?
   c. a combination of a. and b.?

7. If you could live anywhere in the world, would it most likely be . . .
   a. in a large city?
   b. in another country?
   c. in rural America?
   d. at a seaside village?
   e. right where you are now?

8. After you graduate from high school, would your ideal be to . . .
   a. get into summer school and have a jump on college classes in the fall?
   b. work at your usual summer job to save bucks?
   c. take a leisurely vacation around America or another country with a group of friends?
   d. stick pretty close to home, but relax and recreate all summer?

9. What do you find the most relaxing?
   a. Reading or watching a movie.
   b. Jogging or biking.

c. Playing a hard game of tennis or volleyball.
d. Eating a nice dinner out with a group of friends.

10. Which would you most like to learn/do?
    a. Scuba diving.
    b. Gourmet cooking.
    c. Snow/water skiing.
    d. Hang gliding.
    e. None of the above—I like what I do right now.

Tallying Quiz One

Give yourself the following point score for the answers as you chose them:

1. a. 2
   b. 3
   c. 4
   d. 1

2. a. 4
   b. 1
   c. 2
   d. 3

3. a. 4
   b. 5
   c. 2
   d. 3
   e. 1

4. a. 1
   b. 2
   c. 4
   d. 4

5. a. 3
   b. 1
   c. 2
   d. 4

6. a. 1
   b. 3
   c. 2

7. a. 4
   b. 5
   c. 2
   d. 3
   e. 1

8. a. 2
   b. 1
   c. 4
   d. 3

9. a. 1
   b. 3
   c. 4
   d. 2

10. a. 4
    b. 2
    c. 3
    d. 5
    e. 1

Add up your total points and read on:

If you scored 32-42 points, you may tend to take risks that have a fairly high danger factor—either to yourself or those closest to you. It may be wise for you to be sure that you think things through before you go running headlong into situations that may have negative effects on your life.

If you scored 21-31 points, you appear to have a healthy combination of adventuresomeness and sensibility. You probably don't run wildly into danger, yet you'll probably take some risks to get the most out of life. Keep it up!

If you scored 10-20, you may benefit from adding some "spice" to your life by taking a few more chances. Take a class to learn about something you haven't known about before or try a new sport, club or job.

Before any relationship is well grounded, whether with friends, family or as a couple, that part of sharing, caring and loving called "intimacy" must be nurtured. Intimacy is the foundation closeness that a real friendship or true love can be built upon strongly and safely. We'll talk about intimacy next. Knowing the difference between superficial love and real intimacy can make the last part of your passage into adulthood a joyful and exciting experience!

CHAPTER SEVEN

What *Is* Intimacy, Any way?

Kara Johnson sat with her mother, Eve Welsh, in the sunroom of their sprawling suburban home. Eve divorced Kara's father seven years ago, when Kara was ten. Now Eve and Carl Welsh have been married for five years. Eve and Kara had many hurdles to overcome prior to Eve's divorce and in the years since. But, presently, things were going well. Kara felt close to Eve and good about herself. Kara's relationship with Carl had gone from open hostility on her part in the beginning, to cold indifference a couple of years ago, on to a friendly respect now.

Kara's older brother, Josh, is 19 and still working through some deeply-rooted bitterness toward both of his parents and Carl. Josh has been through nearly every phase the television advertisements talk about as they coax families in crisis to call their particular care program for help. Josh has experienced severe depression, gone through a period of smoking marijuana, and drinking alcohol heavily. He's run away from home,

been incarcerated for vandalism, was temporarily suspended from school for fighting on several different occasions, and has broken nearly every rule that Eve has set for him since he began puberty.

Josh's delinquent behavior has caused extreme personal anguish for Eve, his father, Kara, Carl, for Josh himself, and it has placed great stress on their relationships with one another. There have been many confrontations among the group. The interactions between the individuals and within the family have ranged from cold silence to raging anger.

In recent months Carl, Eve, Kara, and Josh have been attending weekly counseling sessions. The topic they are currently discussing is intimacy. They are working on having open communication with each other and sharing their thoughts and feelings honestly.

This morning Kara has some important questions to ask her mother and some urgent matters to discuss. Kara has been dating Phillip most of the past year, and he has been instrumental in helping her see through her family problems. Kara's questions for her mother now have to do with intimacy between a boyfriend and girlfriend, and what part sex plays in intimacy.

Can a couple really be intimate without having sex?

"Mom, I have to ask you something," Kara begins cautiously, "but I don't want you to jump to any conclusions or give me a big lecture. Okay?"

Eve's heart gave a little leap in her chest. What new trauma was she going to have to face now? She deliberately checked a desire to panic, and said slowly, "All right, Kara, what is it?"

"Well," Kara still hesitated. Then she swallowed, and dove into what she was wondering about. "You know at counseling we've been talking about how intimacy means really sharing between people—feelings, thoughts, ideas, love, confidences, and caring. We've said that to be really intimate we have to be open and share our lives with each other. Phillip and I have been talking, Mom, and one of the subjects that always comes up is sex. What I want to ask is, can any couple really be intimate without having sex?"

Eve's heart gave a double leap as all sorts of thoughts raced into her mind. Was Kara trying to say that she and Phillip were having sex? Was Kara pregnant? Did she want Eve to help her get birth control?

Kara watched Eve's face grow tight and turn pale. She groaned inwardly and wished she hadn't asked her mother anything about sex.

But Eve gathered her thoughts quickly and surprised Kara by calmly replying, "I think to answer your question we should look at intimacy in general, and see how important it is to the foundation of any good relationship—couple or otherwise. Then we can look closer at what intimacy means in a sexual relationship."

Kara sighed inside and relaxed in her chair. She and Phillip hadn't had sex yet—mostly because Kara was deeply confused by the many complications that came with her parent's divorce, Eve's remarrying, and Carl's taking a place in their family. Kara thought that sexual attraction was somehow related to people having or not having power over each other. Lately, however, as the family achieved a greater sense of bonding and growth, she had come to see that, in a healthy couple relationship, sex was a mutually shared expression of love and commitment.

This realization freed Kara mentally to consider how she felt about Phillip beyond their close friendship and his great emotional support. Kara could see now that sex with Phillip may not necessarily give him control over her. However, she still sensed that a sexual relationship would still leave her vulnerable in some ways, and she wanted to know what these may be.

Eve interrupted Kara's thoughts to begin answering her questions. "I think, Kara, that what we've been concentrating on in counseling tells us that intimacy is the first, basic requirement for any good relationship. Your unity with friends, parents, teachers, boyfriends, and anyone else who's important to you must begin with some kind of sharing. Intimacy grows from sharing in predictable stages.

"Stage One is when sharing is very casual. Greeting a new friend with, 'Hi! How are you? That's a cute outfit you have on,' are the tiny, first seeds of intimacy.

"Stage Two is when you begin to express how you feel or what you think about what's going on in the world around you. By telling someone what kind of music you like or how you feel about a current event, you are really testing the waters to see if the other person accepts your viewpoints."

"I know," Kara interjected, "like if you can talk about whether you approve of someone *else's* clothes, behavior, or life-style, then it leaves you an escape hatch without risking the other guy's ridicule or criticism. You can personally keep your own beliefs tucked safely inside without exposing them to the other person until you're sure you can trust her!"

"Exactly," Eve affirmed. "Then if you feel safe enough to move deeper into the relationship you are headed into Stage Three.

"Stage Three is when you begin to talk about your own personal tastes, style and experiences. If the other person continues to respect and understand your values and opinions, then you can move on to a more serious relationship.

"Stage Four involves carefully exposing some of your real inner feelings about yourself, your friends and others."

"Uh-huh," Kara nodded, "like when Phillip and I talk about having a fight at home, how I feel when Josh gets into trouble, or what I think about my relationships with Carl and Dad. I think that's the stage I'm in with Phillip. So, is sex the next stage, Mom?"

Eve hesitated only a moment before answering, "Think

about it, Kara. If Phillip was a girlfriend, sex wouldn't be an issue. What do you think the next stage of intimacy would be then?"

"I guess telling each other exactly what you think when you think it—like we do at counseling."

"Right!" Eve said.

"Stage Five is when you can express honestly what you're feeling and know that your whole relationship is not threatened if your feelings are negative. Of course, you shouldn't express your feelings when they may embarrass or purposely hurt the other person. For example, it's not appropriate to expose personal feelings that may shame the other guy in a group. This stage of intimacy does *not* give you the right to be rude, sarcastic or vindictive.

"If you are truly in Stage Five of intimacy you'll usually try everything in your power not to abuse the relationship at all, because that's how deeply you care for the other person. If I can look at Carl and say honestly, 'I resent your trying to tell me how to cope with Josh,' and he can look back at me and openly say, 'I'm only trying to help because I love you,' then we are sharing our real feelings. I call these 'First Lights.' First Lights are any feelings—good or bad—that you can say directly to someone you're very close to. If you're proud of something Phillip's done, then tell him. If you dislike Josh after he's pulled one of his stunts, then you should feel free to let him know that."

"So, when I tell Phillip I'd like to stay home alone one night just because I'm not in the mood to be with him, I'm using First Lights."

"Yes," Eve said, "that's one use. Another may be to say, 'Phillip, one of the reasons I love you so much is because of all the times you've stuck by me during my family crises.' Good or bad aren't really issues with First Lights. Neither are right or wrong. You feel the way you feel. How you choose to act on your feelings is what can make things go smoothly or push them into a breakdown. For instance, withholding feelings of anger will most likely catch up with you by surfacing inappropriately later and hurting everyone involved. On the other hand, missing an opportunity to tell someone he's important to you is a moment that might be lost forever."

"Okay," Kara considered a few seconds, "when two people are truly intimate and they're sharing in all other areas of their lives, what happens when it comes to sex? Is there some invisible wall that's supposed to come up before you act on your feelings to go for it?"

"Not a *wall,* Kara," Eve said, "*thought.* Some good, hard thinking needs to take place about the choices you have about how you act on your feelings. Will you lie about someone who's hurt you? If you do, what might happen? What could the consequences be if you run away because you're angry at home? What will be the result of mouthing off to Carl just because you feel like it? Thought and deliberate choices add up to a much easier life, Kara."

"I'll say!" Kara agreed. "If Josh would've thought about some of the things he's done and made different choices, he would've saved himself and the rest of us a whole lot of grief!"

"That's right," Eve acknowledged, "and that brings up the fact—and there's no way around this—whatever your choices and actions are, they do affect others. That brings me to your question about sex. Choosing to have sex outside of marriage could bring consequences that affect you, Phillip, a baby, your families, and maybe different spouses and children in the future. Does this sound like sex with a boyfriend is necessary in order to be intimate with him?"

Kara grinned at Eve, "No, Mom, I'm not dumb, you know! I see what you mean. Acting on sexual feelings is something you think about and choose how to handle one way or another. No choice *is* a choice!"

"Ah," Eve said, her eyes glistening. "When did my little girl get so grown up?"

"When you were busy trying to keep your life together," Kara said seriously.

"Mmm," Eve responded, "that's for sure. It's been a long haul, Kara, and there will likely be plenty more rough spots ahead. You know I don't regret having been with your father from the standpoint that I have you and Josh. And I love Carl with all my heart. I accept that he's had another life and family that I was not a part of. He loves you kids and I love his three. I hope that by the time all five of you have families of your own, the hurt and heartache of these years will be behind us and we can share our lives just as we are without the extra growing pains. I truly believe that surviving the conflict will make us a stronger, closer family in the end.

"But, I must be totally honest with you, Kara, I wouldn't wish what we've all been through on anyone else. Think, Kara, think. Make your choices about relationships very carefully. Try to choose one husband, one partner, and one best friend all in the same man so that the elements for building a lifetime relationship are there from the very beginning."

"What was missing for you and Dad?" Kara said sincerely.

Eve thought for a moment, "I guess the single most important thing missing was probably just what we've talked about—intimacy. We were in love with the ideas and dreams of love. We assumed that as spouses we would automatically be partners and friends as well. We thought that sex would always be great, money plentiful, and our kids the proof-positive of our undying love. Whoa! Did we have some surprises. We never got past Stage Three of intimacy—our conversations always seemed to dead-end at the point where we discussed how other people did things. We focused on other people so we didn't have to focus on ourselves. We could talk up a storm about how the Smiths treated each other, their kids, and even the cat, but we weren't willing to take the 'log out of our own eyes.' You can't base a lifetime of love on how you feel about the way other people act, Kara, any more than you can base a whole relationship on good sex."

"So you can have sex without intimacy and intimacy without sex," Kara said knowingly.

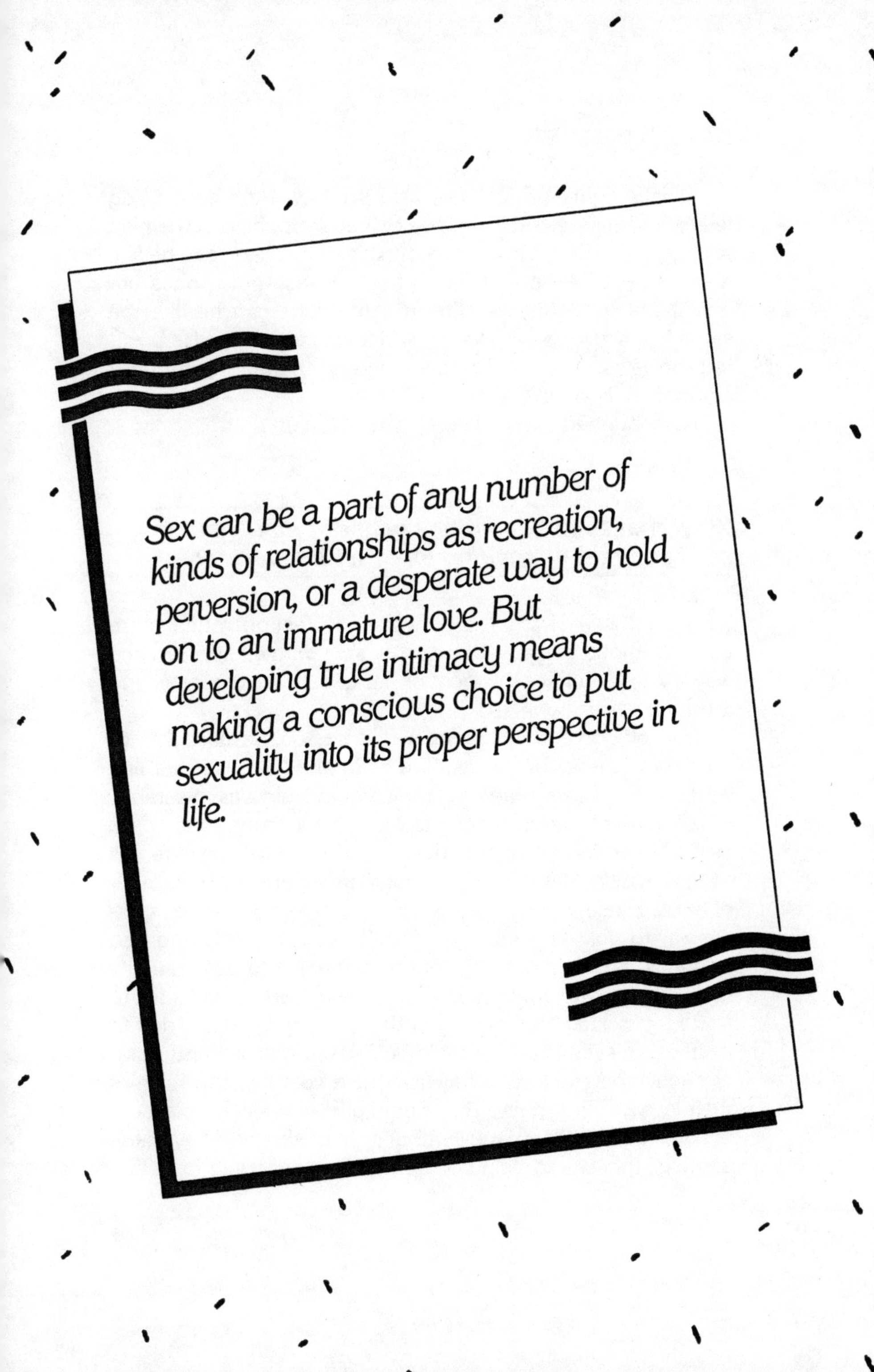
Sex can be a part of any number of
kinds of relationships as recreation,
perversion, or a desperate way to hold
on to an immature love. But
developing true intimacy means
making a conscious choice to put
sexuality into its proper perspective in
life.

"That's right, Kiddo!" Eve said proudly. "And something tells me that you aren't the type to jeopardize having the best relationship you can have! Sex outside of marriage can be like a spark set to paper—it burns hot and fast, but it goes out quick! But a healthy sex life in a marriage can be like the flame in a fireplace—it's warm and toasty as long as it's burning. However, you have to keep feeding the fire, nurturing it along, or it'll go out too."

Kara laughed, "Yeah, I can go with you on that!"

What makes the difference between just "having sex" and really "making love" with a partner?

Kara went away from the conversation feeling much more content about keeping her relationship with Phillip just the way it was. She felt as if most of her questions about sex and intimacy were answered.

Eve felt good about talking with Kara, too. Sexual behavior sure could be full of ironies. Eve hadn't had sex with her first husband before marriage, yet their relationship was miserable. It was not a matter of having sex or not for them. Having sex as God intended within the intimacy of a *sound* marriage was what made the difference! Sex could be a part of any number of kinds of relationships as recreation, perversion, or a desperate way to hold on to an immature love. But developing true intimacy meant making a conscious choice to put sexuality into its proper perspective in life. Eve and Carl had decided to wait for a sexual relationship until after they were married to each other even though they'd both been married and sexually active before. In this way sex was a healthy expression of their love *and* intimacy. They could give and receive pleasure in a healthy new marriage without guilt or shame. They made a choice that would help build a loving relationship for a lifetime!

At what level and with whom can you be really intimate?

After each incident below, circle the letter(s) that corresponds to the person with whom you would be comfortable discussing each incident, choosing from this list:

a. your parents
b. friends of the same sex
c. friends of the opposite sex
d. a steady dating partner
e. a professional, such as a pastor, counselor, or doctor
f. none of these—I'm too private to discuss this
g. any of these—I'm very open about myself

1. Feeling angry about how someone has treated me.
   a b c d e f g

2. Being afraid to try something new. **a b c d e f g**

3. Dreading an important speech, exam, or a big game.
   a b c d e f g

4. Sexual urges or thoughts that I fear are abnormal.
   a b c d e f g

5. An attraction I have to someone of the opposite sex.
   a b c d e f g

6. An awful disappointment such as not getting a part in a play, being the cause of my team's losing a game, or finding out someone I like doesn't like me back.
   a b c d e f g

7. My beliefs in God, including any doubts or tough questions I have about religion. **a b c d e f g**

8. Criticism of the way I've acted. **a b c d e f g**

9. Disapproval of someone else's morals. **a b c d e f g**

10. Someone hurting my feelings. **a b c d e f g**

11. Physical problems, such as menstrual trouble, a lump on a breast or testicle, or unusual discharges from the vagina or penis. **a b c d e f g**

12. Sexual feelings such as tingling, aching, or noticing a heaviness in my groin. **a b c d e f g**

13. Social issues and current events that have to do with politics, the homeless, the hungry, poverty, etc. **a b c d e f g**

14. Contemporary issues that teens face in regard to drugs, alcohol, AIDS, pressure to succeed, etc. **a b c d e f g**

15. Disciplinary rules at home and school. **a b c d e f g**

16. Goals for my future regarding college, career, and family. **a b c d e f g**

17. Mistakes I've made. **a b c d e f g**

18. Dreams and hopes I have that may not seem very realistic right now. **a b c d e f g**

19. Inner fears about things I think others may find silly. **a b c d e f g**

20. Jealousy, resentment, guilt, or other negative emotions.
    a b c d e f g

Tally Up!

In this quiz the most important things to look for are any "all" or "nothing" problems you may be having. For instance, if your answers indicate that you are seldom comfortable discussing things with your parents, then you need to build a bridge across this communication gap. You might show your parents a copy of this quiz and ask them what they think about your not feeling at ease discussing very many topics with them. Or, you may bring up one of the issues that you feel would be the easiest to approach them with and see what happens.

If you indicated that about the only people you can discuss intimate subjects with are friends of the same sex, you may be missing out on sharing more of yourself with friends of the opposite sex, teachers, parents, or other adults in your life. Sharing with a variety of people can add richness to your life and help you to develop the intimacy skills you will need later in a healthy couple relationship.

If you marked almost all your answers with an *f*, it may be wise for you to stop and think through how you feel about the people in your life. Human beings are social creatures and we inherently need to tell our thoughts and feelings to others sometimes. We are all interconnected somehow through our jobs, parents, siblings, schools, churches, or neighborhoods. If you find that you're not able to communicate intimately with anyone, you may be experiencing loneliness. Try very hard to reach out to someone. Begin by talking about an "easy" topic, such as an upcoming school event, then gradually work into a closer friendship when you feel safer. It takes practice to become more outgoing. If you're going through serious depression or extreme anxiety, please ask an adult for help! You can overcome your isolation. But you are the only one who knows for sure that you need to approach others for help.

Most people are thankful for the opportunity to aid someone who sincerely needs guidance.

If you circled a lot of *g,*'s indicating that you are open about yourself, then it would appear that you are healthy and well-adjusted in the area of intimacy. If you feel comfortable talking with your teachers about problems at home, for instance, but not with your parents, don't worry; this is very common during adolescence. If you fear that some of your sexual thoughts are abnormal, but can only bring yourself to say something to friends of the same sex, that's okay. Just remember that your friends only have about as much experience in life as you do and you may need to talk to a trusted adult to get real relief from your fears. And if you feel that you are too private a person to discuss your sexuality with others, then that's fine as long as it doesn't cause you worry or concern.

How and with whom you relate is totally a matter of personal style. You may feel more comfortable relating with one or two very close friends. Or you may be in your element in a group. It doesn't matter which, as long as you feel good about yourself overall. You need only be concerned when your intimate relationships seem to cause you or others great pain. Then it's time to closely examine what's going on with you, and possibly to reach out for help.

Being truly intimate rarely comes without practice and effort. In fact, it can be downright work. But it's nearly always worth it because of the depth and joy it adds to our lives!

Teens often have lots of questions about what's normal, when it comes to their sexuality and couple relationships. You may have concerns regarding everything from how often you should kiss to whether homosexuality is normal. Some people these days, especially in the entertainment industry, dress as the opposite sex. Others take steroids and hormones that blur sexual differences. Although some people may assume that all this is harmless, it's not quite true. Equality of the sexes is one thing; *sameness* is a completely different story.

God created males and females so their differences could be appreciated—not for them to try to turn themselves into the same sex. To do so can be confusing and threatening to a person who is trying to develop strong self-esteem. A "unisex" life-style can erode a clear-headed acceptance of one's sexuality.

These days there are many flamboyantly gay men and women, as well as large numbers of "closet" homosexual men and lesbians. Growing up with acute awareness of homosexuality has caused many contemporary teens great anxiety over what's normal and what's not, when it comes to their sexual choices. Next we will discuss homosexuality, and the fears that can surround it.

CHAPTER EIGHT

Are You "Normal"? Gay?

Allen, 18, has some concerns about what is normal sexually for teens his age. Fortunately, he is very close to Kyle, a youth worker at the church Allen has grown up in. Allen respects Kyle, who is in his 30s, married, and a good Christian leader. Allen approached Kyle while the two cleaned up after a youth group activity one evening.

"I'd like to ask you about some things that have been bothering me, Kyle," Allen said.

Kyle took one look at Allen and knew this was major stuff. "Sure. What is it?"

Allen put down the folding chair he had been about to put away and sat on it. He looked Kyle directly in the eyes and said, "I'm scared. I've been living with some pretty big questions running around in my head for quite awhile and I don't know how to deal with them by myself. I've tried, but I just

can't seem to come up with any answers. You've known me all through junior high and high school, Kyle, so I figure you can help me sort this out as well as anyone."

"Sure, Allen," Kyle said. "You don't have to worry—you can ask me anything!"

"This one might shock you." Allen hesitated several seconds, searching for a delicate way to come to the point. Finding no tactful words for his question he blurted, "I'm afraid I'm gay!"

Kyle's face fell for a moment and then he leaned on the broom he had been pushing and burst into nervous laughter. "Whatever in the world makes you think that?!"

Allen's face showed alarm at Kyle's reaction. He attempted to withdraw by becoming defensive. "If you think it's so funny, then just forget it!"

Kyle sobered immediately. "I'm sorry, Allen. I didn't mean to hurt your feelings. I just wasn't expecting you to ask about anything at all like homosexuality. Seriously, what makes you feel you might be gay?"

Allen's great need to deal with his pain and concern overrode any wariness he may have otherwise had in seeking help. He was gravely solemn as he spoke. "First, because I'm 18 and I haven't even dated! I mean, I went with a girl to the prom and I hang out with a group of guys and girls, but I haven't actually dated anyone. And, worse, I haven't even been really attracted to any girls."

"You mean you haven't felt *sexually* attracted to girls?" Kyle asked.

"Yeah. The other guys have been drooling over girls since seventh and eighth grades. They're always talking about the girls' figures and making jokes about getting together with them on dates and stuff."

"And how do you feel when the other guys talk like this?"

"I don't know," Allen shook his head in confusion. "Not like they do—I know that much! I think girls in general are nice. I think they're pretty and all, but I can't really picture me with a girl sexually. And all the other guys tease me about being weird and *gay!*

"Do you literally mean all the guys, Allen, or do you mean a handful of them?" Kyle questioned.

Allen considered for several seconds, ticking off names in his mind. "I guess it's just three or four guys that have lockers near mine," he said.

"And why do you feel that these three or four guys have a handle on girls and sexuality?"

"Aw, Kyle, give me a break!" Allen exclaimed. "Look at all the movies, magazines, and television—everything is about sex!"

"And you think guys are reacting to all the sex around them?"

"Well, yes!" Allen responded.

"Have you ever acted brave when you were really scared to death inside?"

"Yeah," Allen answered cautiously. "So?"

"So, didn't you act brave because you thought that was the way you were expected to react?

Allen nodded and Kyle continued, "So, isn't it possible that the other guys drool over girls and act like they know all about sex because they think that's how they're expected to act? Or maybe so that other people around them will think they're more experienced than they really are?"

"I suppose that's possible, but they do go on dates and they seem to fit in with the way things are supposed to be."

"Who defines the way things are supposed to be?" Kyle still probed.

"I guess the media," Allen said. "And people."

"The media—okay—then do you think the other guys believe what they see in the movies and on television? And do you think that you should believe it too?"

"I s'pose so. I mean why would they show the things they show to regular people if regular people didn't want what they see?" Allen quizzed Kyle.

"How about because successful marketers know how to sell people on the idea that 'in order to be successful and loved you have to be sexy and in order to be sexy you have to buy our client's product or service'? You know, Allen, society in general, but teens especially, are victims of a constant media blitz. Beer companies reel in their next generation of drinkers by bombarding us with ads having sexy men and women laughing at bars, on the beach, and in other seductive situations. Sex sells products and services!

"But it also sells people some very false images! Eating disorders such as anorexia nervosa and bulimia are very common, largely because of the media's false impression that the only 'normal' figure is tall and thin.[1] There are thousands of drug and alcohol addicts who think they must get high to have fun and belong. And there are those who are addicted to fast times, fast cars, and fast money. People are becoming indifferent to the ideas of unisex and homosexuality, and are accepting these things as 'normal' in growing numbers."

"Right!" declared Allen. "If you're not into sexy male and female relationships, then people think you're gay!"

"But don't you see, Allen? That's part of the false image! The guys who give you a hard time believe the sex propaganda, and you're comparing yourself with them when they're role-playing something that isn't even reality in the first place! Just because your feelings don't fit in with the images that other people project, or your biological and emotional time clocks don't go along with the average teen's, doesn't mean that you're abnormal. It simply means that you're normal for you!"

"At 18?" Allen asked doubtfully. "If I'm not attracted to girls yet, there must be the possibility that I'm gay!"

"You know," said Kyle, "as I mentioned before, people accept things like homosexuality more these days than they used to. That means it's a choice that's more readily available for people to make. It's easier for some who fall outside of the accepted norm to choose to give in to a gay life-style."

"*Choose* to be gay?" Allen could hardly believe what he was hearing. "Who would want to make that choice?"

"Ah, Allen," Kyle said slowly, "homosexuality *is* a choice. There are all kinds of reasons why people may fall into a gay life-style. Maybe underlying personality problems that come from a dysfunctional background, or not fitting into what society at large believes is normal, like where your fears stem from. It's even possible that a deeply-rooted rebellion against parents or society expresses itself in homosexuality.

"Society's emphasis on sexual interaction, combined with our acceptance of homosexuality, feeds into an unreal or abstract image that some people have of themselves. And before they even realize what has happened, they may fall into a homosexual encounter. Then, once an encounter has occurred, not only is the abstract self-image reinforced, but guilt, shame, and fear multiply unbelievably fast. These destructive emotions feed into each other also, and more quickly than you might think. Soon people have labeled themselves permanently as homosexuals before they even know what hit 'em. In reality they may have been just like you, a healthy, normal—and I do mean *normal*—young man or woman who's been confused by the media messages that are allowed to run rampant, and the reactions of their peers to these messages."

"I still don't get why you think it's a choice—subconscious or deliberate," Allen prodded.

"Well," Kyle put his broom against a wall, "let me get a Bible and we'll look at a couple of Scriptures."

Kyle checked the concordance at the back of his Bible and quickly thumbed to Leviticus 20:13. "Here it says, 'If a man lies with a man as one lies with a woman, both of them have done what is detestable.' And Romans 1:26 and 27 says, 'Women exchanged natural relations for unnatural ones. In the same way the men also abandoned natural relations with women and were inflamed with lust for one another.'

"This shows us clearly that the natural sexual

relationship—God's plan—is between men and women. To act unnaturally involves a choice, Allen. Think about it. God wouldn't create us to do something unnatural or detestable. If we are involved in unnatural activities it is because we choose to do that which is not beneficial to us. It is not natural for us to do anything that is harmful to us if we are working toward developing the character of Christ. But, humans that we are, we often make choices that are destructive. The only way we can meet Christ and turn our lives around is by opening the doorway to our hearts."

"Kyle," Allen interrupted, "before you go on, I have to tell you one more thing. I haven't had any physical contacts, but I have to confess that I've felt sexual admiration for other guys."

If I think someone of the same sex is attractive, does that mean I may be gay?

Kyle watched with compassion as Allen winced at his own words. "That doesn't sound so odd to me. To look at someone who may be your ideal of masculinity and admire that, or to appreciate the sensuality of what you find attractive in your same sex, seems okay to me. Look at the admiration among men toward professional athletes, or the appreciation among women for the beautiful figures or features of professional models. In many ways these types of attractions are more channels for daydreams than anything else.

"Now, admittedly, to *dwell* on this type of attraction can bring on a lot of other problems. Obsession with the same sex or lust toward members of your gender does need to be gotten rid of as quickly as possible. You always have a choice to go with an open heart to God and confess your lust in Jesus' name. Not only can you be forgiven, but you can literally be empowered by the Holy Spirit to change your attitudes.

"You must bear in mind, Allen, that as a teenager you are intensely vulnerable to what society feeds your mind about sexuality. Teens can emotionally fall into a choice of homosexuality by feeling as you started out feeling—fearful, insecure, doubtful, ashamed, guilty, confused, and like the odd man out. Had you not found the courage to ask someone you trusted about your concerns, things may have snowballed on you. Maybe someone who has made a choice to be gay, and is more experienced than you, could have seduced you into an encounter by preying on your doubts and insecurities.

"Or, say you got involved with drugs or alcohol and fell into a homosexual encounter while your inhibitions were absent—this would water the seeds of doubt that were already planted within you. Your feelings of fear and confusion would add more water to the weeds that sprouted. Before you knew it, another encounter may happen and—boom—this could be all the confirmation you need to convince yourself that you're gay."

"So you're saying that the *ingredients* were there for me to push myself over the edge into a gay life-style, but that really isn't me at all?"

"Exactly, Allen. Normal is whatever fits you like a glove that was made for you by God himself. If it feels comfortable and doesn't go directly against God's plan, then it is right for you. My feeling is very certain—you are simply a late bloomer. Your sexual maturity is merely a little behind that of your peers, that's all. Right now other things are more important to you, such as school, work and your family. You will begin to feel attractions for girls when your mind and body are ready—despite what the media shoves in your face! For now, you can keep your eyes on what is healthy and natural. Paul's prayer in Ephesians 1:18 is that 'the eyes of your heart may be enlightened in order that you may know the hope to which he has called you, the riches of his glorious inheritance.' God's riches and calling do not have anything to do with the unnatural or detestable—only good."

As Kyle spoke, Allen relaxed in his seat. The relief was apparent on his face. "Whew!" he said. "I'm glad I brought this

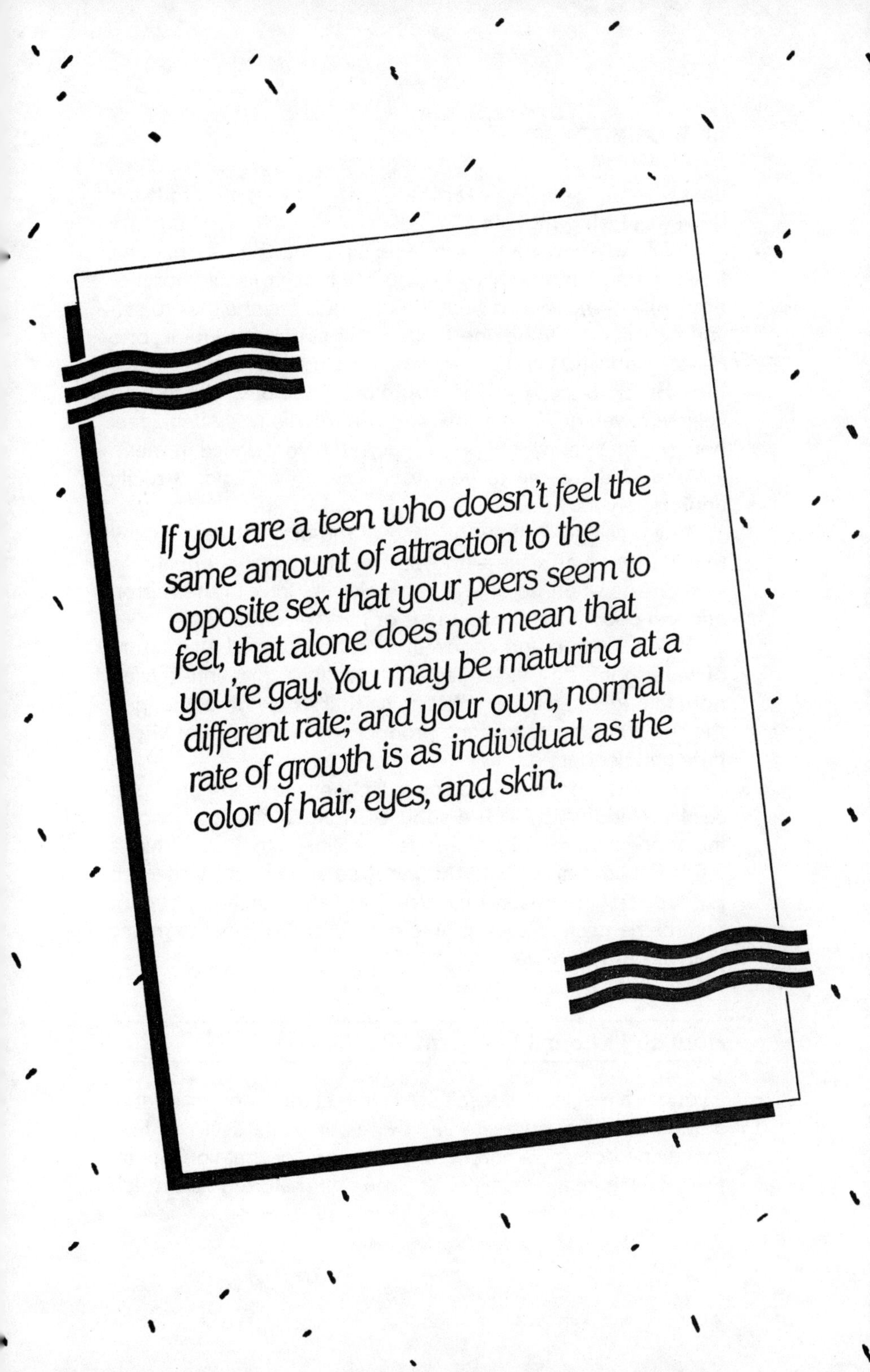

If you are a teen who doesn't feel the same amount of attraction to the opposite sex that your peers seem to feel, that alone does not mean that you're gay. You may be maturing at a different rate; and your own, normal rate of growth is as individual as the color of hair, eyes, and skin.

up. I was really getting near the edge! I was starting to think that I was losing my mind."

"Well, whenever a person feels like that, there's only one true source of finding his way. You can figure this for your lifetime, Allen—no matter what bill of goods anyone tries to sell you—there's got to be one Truth in this world, one Guide, one Master plan, and I can assure you, it's God! You can count on Him, His Son, the Holy Spirit, and the Body of Christ to help keep you well-grounded. I'm glad you trusted me, Allen. I feel honored that you would place that much confidence in me."

"I'm glad I came to you, too, Kyle," Allen said. "I really appreciate your help."

"My privilege. I know that one of the greatest days in any man's or woman's life—and all I've said applies equally to women—is when he or she can wake up, look in the mirror, and feel good about living in his or her own skin!"

Kyle's wisdom and counseling probably saved Allen years of pain, grief, and struggles. It most likely prevented Allen from falling into a miserable choice that would have changed the entire course of a bright, productive life into one of bitterness and heartache.

Of course, not every person will choose to marry and have sexual relationships with a spouse. There is absolutely nothing wrong with remaining single or celibate. In 1 Corinthians 7:8-9, Paul explains about the widowed and the unmarried: "It is good for them to stay unmarried, as I am. But if they cannot control themselves, they should marry, for it is better to marry than to burn with passion."

How do I know if I'm normal?

If you are a teen who doesn't seem to feel the same amount of attraction to the opposite sex that your peers seem to feel, that alone does not mean that you're gay, or that you'll positively be single all your life! You may be maturing at a much different rate than some kids your age; and your own, *normal* rate of growth is as individual as the color of hair, eyes, and skin.

Remember that normal is what feels good and right for you from within yourself, and what is in keeping with God's will. You know how you feel inside when you've done something wrong—perhaps lied or cheated—and you know how you feel inside when you're living right—full of smiles, hope, and love.

You realize that if you deliberately do something against your parents or friends you don't feel normal about it. You may feel angry, guilty, ashamed, or vengeful; most people rarely feel great when they do real wrong. When you do feel a pang of conscience over a wrong decision, try to recognize that it is your built-in warning system. Don't get in the habit of ignoring these feelings. This is essential to your walking a wonderful, adventurous journey through life with God. The conscience you feel is the Holy Spirit trying to guide and protect you.

In John 14:26 Jesus promises that the "Counselor, the Holy Spirit, whom the Father will send in my name, will teach you all things and will remind you of everything I have said to you." When you are confused, wondering about making a choice that falls into an area that you have some misgivings about, but have no real black and white rules to follow, the Holy Spirit can be counted on to help you through your confusion. Romans 8:26 says, "The Spirit helps us in our weakness. We do not know what we ought to pray for, but the Spirit himself intercedes for us with groans that words cannot express."

If you, like Allen, are worried about your sexual development and preferences or about the future of your relationships, bear in mind that not every moment of every day is going to be totally free of pain, doubt, or confusion. This world is not perfect. You must face the fact that you *will* have to make tough decisions throughout your lifetime; it is inevitable. But if you are striving to live close to God's ways you can *know* that you will be all right. It is important that you also know that, with an attitude of willingness to meet trials and suffering head-on, any painful situation can become an opportunity to grow.

Will God help me make choices?

When you make painful, damaging choices, there is always a way to get yourself right again—you can turn to God in confidence through His Son, Jesus Christ. Jesus gives us God's promise in Hebrews 13:5: "Never will I leave you, never will I forsake you."

God doesn't take vacations. He's always there for you. He doesn't sulk and withhold His love when you do something wrong. God doesn't force His ways on you, even though they're the right ones. He leaves your choices up to you. When you are afraid or tempted, you can count on Him to help you through if you'll only ask.

It's important to note that there's a big difference between what you're tempted to do and the choices you are forced to make in unexpected circumstances. Temptations are the things you want to do to please yourself but know you shouldn't—like eating too many sweets. Situations you find yourself in all of a sudden, that force you to make a choice, usually involve what others want you to do—such as to have sex.

It is vital that you don't overestimate your capacity to "go it alone" in dangerous situations. God gives you the ability to overcome temptations, but He also gives you free will and won't likely interfere with your paying the consequences of poor choices. Hopefully, the consequences you pay will help you learn not to make destructive choices again.

There is a dark side to human sexuality involving our selfish desires. Satan will fight to get us to follow him with very deadly weapons! He may play on our insecurities, fears, depressions, or whatever else he can sense that we are vulnerable to. We must be watchful.

The dark side of human sexuality is not pleasant. In fact, many loving parents hesitate to talk about things such as rape, incest, molestations, the horrors of a drug-infested life, and pornography. They hope that their children never have to know about such violent things. And they certainly hope that their kids will never be personally exposed to such ugly circumstances.

Unfortunately, most of today's teens do know about such things. To avoid discussing and learning about them is to leave you unarmed at a time when you may need to protect yourself from people who may try to force or mesmerize you into their own dark worlds.

Christian kids are not immune to the darker issues of the world. In fact, they are perfect targets because of their bubbling love of life and others. You may learn from the next chapter how to spot dangerous circumstances, and discover some ways to protect yourself from messing up big time! First, let's look at whether or not *guilt* is interfering with your life. Guilt simply means that you are feeling responsible for doing wrong. Healthy guilt is God's way of leading you to put things right. But feeling guilty for a long period of time over what's in the past can be a poisonous emotion and is usually unnecessary.

Are you living with unnecessary guilt?

Put a check beside each action that makes (or would make) you feel guilty:

1. Leaving your room a mess. ____

2. Swearing. ____

3. Mouthing off to your parents. _____

4. Telling a small lie to get out of something you don't want to do. _____

5. Telling a small lie to avoid hurting someone else's feelings. _____

6. Gossiping. _____

7. Getting bad grades. _____

8. Cheating on a test. _____

9. Getting a haircut your parents don't like. _____

10. Wearing clothes your parents hate. _____

11. Showing poor effort in an individual sport like swimming or wrestling. _____

12. Performing poorly in a team sport such as volleyball or football. _____

13. Saying that you would baby-sit or mow the lawn for someone and then just not show up. _____

14. Telling your parents that you did an errand or a task, which you really didn't do, to escape being disciplined. _____

15. Getting home a half hour late from a date. _____

16. Overhearing your parents argue or make love. _____

17. Getting a younger brother or sister in trouble on

purpose in order to get them back for something he/she did to you. ____

18. Secretly belonging to a club you know your parents disapprove of. ____

19. Washing your mom's new sweater with the "hot water" clothes and ruining it. ____

20. Hiding the fact that you ruined your mom's new sweater. ____

21. Forgetting to ask God to forgive you for something you did that you know is wrong. ____

22. Telling someone he/she looks good in an outfit that really makes him/her look horrible. ____

23. Telling a kid on your basketball team that he/she did a great job when he/she really did terribly, but you know the kid did the best he/she could. ____

24. Listening in on another's phone conversation. ____

25. Knowing you didn't try your best on a big exam at school or a special job assignment. ____

Tally Up!
Count the number of items you checked and read on.

If you checked fewer than five items, it is very likely that you are making a bid for attention from your parents, peers, or teachers by behaving inappropriately. You may be crying for help without being aware of it. If you are doing many things that you know in your mind are not right, yet you don't regret them, then you need to stop and evaluate your attitudes and feelings. Can you see any pattern in what you're doing? For instance, do most of the things you checked have to do with your relationship to your parents (rebelling by getting in late, lying to them, mouthing off a lot)? Are you acting disrespectfully to your peers (gossiping about others, eavesdropping on conversations, starting rumors)? Or, have you been involved in something that you feel so badly about (drugs, sexual misconduct, stealing, etc.) that you're trying to harden yourself by feeling guilt over other, more everyday types of things?

It is vital for your future adjustment to adulthood and happiness that you stop right now and work on behaving in ways that contribute to a clear conscience. Seek the help of a school counselor, pastor, teacher, parent, coach, or other responsible adult. Regardless of what you may or may not have done, you can clean the slate! Plant the following Scripture deep within you: "If we confess our sins, he is faithful and just and will forgive us our sins and purify us from all unrighteousness" (1 John 1:9).

If you checked between 5 and 15 items, it is likely that you feel the Holy Spirit convicting you (making you aware) of the wrong things you do. You probably have a well-balanced sense of justice and a healthy conscience that is guiding you through the final phase of your passage into adulthood. By knowing what you've done wrong, confessing it to yourself and to God, and changing your behavior, you can rest assured that you'll be all right! Everyone does wrong at times and there is no need to suffer with guilt that eats away at your self-esteem. For instance, many teens live with guilt over tensions at home during adolescence, when in reality some of this friction is necessary. If there wasn't a "pulling away" and a testing, a teen would have no reason to grow independent of his/her parents. Many parents have trouble understanding this, too. They worry or may downright panic over a teen who always seems to be challenging them. But the pushing and tugging are often necessary to help loosen the deep bonds of childhood so that parents and teens can begin to form healthy adult relationships between each other. So, keep on letting your conscience guide you, and informing your conscience with God's Word. But don't let guilt take over if you go through a period when you feel that you just can't do anything right.

If you checked more than 15 items and you're truly feeling guilty, then you may be in need of some real help. Could it be that you're living in a home that places too many expectations on you? Do you put too many expectations on yourself? Is there something else wrong in your life? For example, many kids feel so much misplaced guilt and worry over their parents' divorce that they begin to think that the split is their fault or that by being a "perfect" kid the parents may get back together. It is *not* true that children cause divorce! Parents are adults who must live with their choices. Only they decide to split their marriage and family—not the kids. Of course, there is no such thing as a perfect kid or adult. No matter how "good" you are you will not reach perfection. If this is the type of guilt you're living with, stop right now and talk to someone outside your family about your feelings. Let them know how hard you may be taking a divorce, illness at home, or the results of an accident that couldn't be avoided. Someone who isn't closely related to you may be more objective and may be able to help you to see what's realistic about how you're handling your guilt and what's unrealistic about the burden you are carrying.

You might show a teacher, friend, or counselor this quiz and go over why you feel so guilty about the items you checked. This will probably open up doors to different aspects of what's going on in your life and help you to communicate things out loud that may only need expression to free you from your concerns. Don't worry—you're going to be okay!

Remember this: Guilt means to be responsible for something. The only "guilty" feelings you need to have are ones that make you aware that you are responsible for doing something wrong or hurtful. Dragging out feelings of guilt after you have acknowledged your wrong, asked God to forgive you, and changed your behavior is totally unnecessary!

You maybe wondering what *does* happen when you really mess up—or what to do about it after you have. We'll see how this can be handled in the next chapter.

CHAPTER NINE

Messing Up Majorly!

Ingrid was 19 when she did some things she thought God could never forgive her for. It started very innocently. She went to a party with Gene who was in his senior year in college. She met Gene at the fast-food restaurant where she worked and was immediately infatuated with him. It never occurred to her that Gene would put her in any danger. But when they walked into the house where the party was being held, Ingrid knew right away that it was wrong for her to be there. A foggy film of marijuana smoke hung in the air, there was a bowl of brightly-colored pills in the middle of a coffee table and lines of cocaine waiting to be sniffed on the kitchen counter.

Gene introduced Ingrid to several young people who hovered on the back deck around a keg of beer. They looked skeptically at Ingrid standing under a light with clear eyes and an alert, cautious expression. Gene assured the group that

Ingrid was okay, and they seemed to take his word. Ingrid accepted a glass of beer someone offered her, thinking to herself that she would sip on it while she decided how she could best get out of this delicate situation.

Gene was 22, extremely handsome, popular, and seemed to be highly respected by his peers. Ingrid, on the other hand, was having trouble adjusting to her freshman year of college, feeling awkward, insecure, and without having made any good friends since leaving home. She desperately wanted approval and to feel that she fit into a new, adult life-style. Ingrid felt safe with Gene, and thought that having a relationship with him might help her ease into college life.

Can "good Christian kids" fall into real *trouble?*

Gene seemed proud and happy to have Ingrid at his side. He was courteous and considerate to include her as they visited with the other kids. He introduced her to all of his friends as the newest entree in their group, and everyone laughed. Ingrid took this as acceptance and was flattered. Next thing she knew she had drunk three glasses of beer while she was supposedly trying to decide how to get out of mixing too heavily with the crowd.

When Gene offered her a joint that was being passed around the circle, she looked at him with wide-eyed fear. She had never tried marijuana, and every alarm bell was sounding within her to get away from the party before it was too late. Gene slipped his arm around her, though, and gently coaxed her to inhale from the joint by telling her that he would never do anything to hurt someone he really cared about. The implication that she was just such a person, combined with the mellowing effects of the beer, prompted Ingrid to drop her guard a moment too long. Gene saw the waiver in her constitution and leaned over to give her a seductive, passion-filled kiss on the mouth. This melted Ingrid's resolve and she drew the next puff of smoke into her lungs thinking that perhaps she was just being a baby and afraid to run with the fast crowd. She assured herself that Gene's words were true and he wouldn't do anything to hurt her.

Several joints later, with puffs taken from each at varying intervals, Ingrid was flying. She felt sexy and confident. Gene was going back and forth between drinking beer and inhaling from the joints—and grabbing at Ingrid. He was kissing her, hugging her, and looking at her with increased lust.

All of a sudden Gene shouted, "Hey, Everyone! It's time for some real partying—to the candy in the kitchen, kids!"

A burst of loud laughter rang out in the cool night as everyone followed Gene into the house through the sliding glass doors. It took Ingrid's mind several seconds to realize that Gene was telling them that it was time to use cocaine. A brief vision of the Pied Piper flashed through Ingrid's mind as the Holy Spirit tried once again to warn her against the very real dangers of blindly following someone just because he seemed to be singing a good tune. Ingrid, however, was too far away from her normal senses. She simply pushed the vision out of her mind and went into the kitchen. A pretty girl was squealing, "Ooh! This is such a happening party, Gene!" just as Ingrid walked up behind the group. Maybe she would just watch them.

However, Gene was soon enticing Ingrid to step up to the counter and just try a little coke. She gave into the temptation to feel "even better" than she already did. Ingrid placed a finger against one side of her nose, leaned into the white powder on the glass slide with the other nostril and sniffed up what she could in one snort. It was a funny, foreign feeling, not entirely pleasant to her. But a few moments later Ingrid did feel entirely pleasant—in fact, euphoric. She felt a complete sense of well-being.

Ingrid lost all sense of time then and wasn't sure how long it was before she realized that Gene was no longer in the kitchen. A tiny sense of panic prickled at the back of her neck and she wandered into the living room to look for him. He wasn't there. She looked out on the back deck, but he wasn't there, either. The feeling of panic was growing and Ingrid was beginning to feel like Cinderella at midnight. Would she soon turn into a pumpkin? The thought hit her as hilarious and she roared in laughter as she made her way down a hallway to find the bathroom.

Ingrid was finishing up washing her hands when she found herself gazing into the mirror at her own reflection. The effects of the cocaine were wearing off quickly. She felt buoyed only by the marijuana and alcohol that was still in her system. Oh! She had to find Gene! She wanted that illusive euphoria back!

Ingrid turned into the hallway and opened each door that she passed. Three bedrooms had couples in varying stages of undress in them. A fourth room was an empty office. Ingrid opened the fifth door just a crack, noticing that it opened onto a large, master bedroom suite. She was shocked to find Gene in bed with a dark-haired girl. Gene did not notice Ingrid watching through the slightly open door. She was at once filled with anger and fascination. She hated what she was seeing, yet she couldn't tear her eyes away.

Ingrid leaned a little too hard on the door as she watched the couple and literally fell into the room. Gene didn't appear to be disturbed at all by her presence. He looked over at Ingrid casually and smiled, "Hey, babe! Where've you been?"

"Uh," Ingrid stammered, amazed at his lack of modesty or concern. "Uh, I was out at the party."

"Aaah," Gene grinned more widely, "and I bet you need another little lift of the nose candy! C'mere, and I'll get you some!"

Ingrid was walking a line so dangerous and destructive that she couldn't begin to understand how close she was to falling into a deep pit of shame and despair. At the very moment, however, all she could manage for feelings was relief that Gene still noticed her, and a driving curiosity to see more of what was going on. She walked slowly toward the bed. In

Ingrid's hazy mind it seemed to take forever to reach Gene's outstretched hand.

"C'mon, little one." Gene said as he rolled over and sat up cross-legged. He nodded at the dark-haired girl with some invisible communication and she stood up, picked up her clothes, and left. Gene reached for a tiny silver cylinder on the night stand and, seconds later, Ingrid was sitting on the bed facing Gene, snorting more cocaine. Soon, Gene was leaning over, fondling her breasts and kissing her mouth with a probing tongue. The euphoric effects of the drug gripped Ingrid completely and she knew only that her mind wanted her body to keep feeling good. As Gene removed Ingrid's clothes she experienced a brief feeling that she was doing wrong and should stop!

That was Ingrid's last contact with reality until she pulled herself awake the next morning.

Half-conscious, Ingrid hoped with all her being that the murky thoughts filtering into her mind were from a nightmare rather than memory and that when she opened her eyes she would be in her own, clean dorm room. However, as she pried herself away from the vice-like clamp of sleep, a growing terror filled her heart. What had she done?! All at once she remembered, and flew into a sitting position. She sat amid a pile of bedding that was unfamiliar to her, in the middle of a bed that was not her own.

How can I face myself, others, and God when I've really *messed up?*

A feeling of complete repulsion overtook Ingrid. She began shaking, and she buried her face in her hands. Wave after wave of nausea swept over her. She tumbled off the bed, staggered across the floor and into a bathroom where she vomited violently again and again. How she wished she could throw up all the things she had done last night and flush them away.

After her body's wrenching quieted to trembling despair, Ingrid pulled herself up by holding onto the edge of the vanity. Looking into a gilt-edged mirror, she came face-to-face with the reality of herself. The gray face and swollen eyes, capped by a crop of messy, blond hair, were barely recognizable. Leaning on the vanity to hold herself up, Ingrid cried, "Oh, God! What have I done to myself?!"

A picture of her stern-faced father, standing in the pulpit of the church he ministered to, crowded in on Ingrid. She could hear his voice, extolling the virtues of doing right and pleading with his congregation to be moral. She clamped a hand over each ear to try to make her father's voice go away, and she squeezed her eyes tightly shut to dispel his image.

Ingrid had never imagined that anyone, except maybe murderers, could feel so dirty and disgusting. She turned and slammed the bathroom door as hard as she could. She shoved the lock into place and stepped into a tiled shower. She put the water on as hard as she could stand it and stood under the spray.

When Ingrid's mind cleared from the depressed sleep brought on by drugs and alcohol, she felt even worse than before. She had given away her virginity while she was in a stupor last night—to someone she barely knew! What would she do? Where could she go? Should she simply do away with herself? Certainly, she thought, she had ruined her life beyond repair. Drinking, smoking dope, snorting cocaine, and having sex all in one sweep was the most horrible thing Ingrid could think of for a young, previously innocent girl to do.

She was certain that no one could have an ounce of compassion for her after what she had let happen to her. And she doubted she could live with it inside. Then, of course, Gene knew what had gone on. So did God. Suicide became plausible in Ingrid's mind. This would be a way to avoid *ever* having to face Gene, that dark-haired girl, Ingrid's parents, anyone else, and herself again!

No other option came to Ingrid as she shut the shower off

and grabbed a towel from a shelf. Her heart pounded rapidly and she felt light-headed as she resolved to go back to her dorm room and think about what to do.

Deep sadness enveloped Ingrid as she dressed. She stepped quietly from the bedroom, preparing to sneak out of the house. But she could tell that the house was empty by the complete stillness that greeted her. She walked down the hallway and peeked around the corner into the living room and beyond to the dining area. She stepped into the foyer to leave, but something compelled her to walk back into the kitchen area and look out onto the deck. Ingrid was surprised to see that the house was amazingly neat for all the carousing that had gone on last night. She looked up at a clock on the wall above the kitchen cabinets and was also surprised to see that it read four o'clock. She had slept nearly the whole day away!

As Ingrid turned to leave, a note held onto the refrigerator by a magnet caught her eye. She leaned closer and read it: "To Whom It May Concern: We've gone for lunch, then on to play golf and we'll be back later with the goods to do some serious partying! Love ya, Gene."

Ingrid nearly gagged. The seemingly innocent words could just as well have meant that a group of friends had gone to share a meal, play together and return later to have food, sodas and a dance. So much destructiveness disguised in such happy words!

Ingrid grabbed the note, tore it into bits and pieces and tossed them into the air. How many other people had been lured into doing things against their normal wills by drugs and too much alcohol? How many would come after her? And how much worse could it have been? Ingrid couldn't think of anything worse right now. Instead, with self-loathing, she thought of how she'd acted.

In fact, she was thoroughly convinced, as she walked dejectedly down the sidewalk, that she was the most worthless girl in the world. As she passed by the campus chapel a sense of shame overwhelmed her heart. She stopped at the end of the walk that led to the chapel's doors and gazed up at the sun-sparkled, stained-glass window above. The portrayal of Christ etched in the window seemed to come alive before her eyes and beckon to her. She inched up the walk without even realizing what she was doing. Ingrid got to the bottom of the cement steps and her legs folded beneath her. She crumpled to the ground like a forgotten rag doll.

The pain, remorse, and fear surrounding her own human vulnerability welled up inside her and hot tears began streaming down her face. Her tears turned into gushing sobs as she rocked back and forth, wishing she could erase the last 24 hours of her life.

From the garden at the side of the chapel, Pastor Lewis heard a whimpering, whining sound that he thought might be a wounded animal. The elderly pastor went to see what he could do, and found Ingrid in a small heap on the chapel steps.

He bent over and put his hands under the young woman's arms. "Come," he said gently, "come with me inside and tell me what's the matter."

Ingrid suddenly turned on the robed man as violently as though she really were a wounded animal. "No!" she cried hysterically. "I can't go in there! I'm not worth your time! Pastor, I've done the most horrible, awful things! I just want to die!"

Pastor Lewis had been the campus chaplain for nearly 20 years. He had ministered to young women who had tried to give themselves abortions, prostituted their bodies, used heroin and just about any other drug one could think of; there were those who had been the victims of incest or molestation, and those who had committed almost every imaginable sin. He doubted that this slip of a girl could tell him anything that would shock him, and he knew for sure that there was nothing so big that God couldn't handle it.

"What is your name?" Pastor Lewis asked softly.

"Ingrid."

"Well, Ingrid," the pastor offered, "I want to give you one Scripture quickly and hope you will then come into the chapel with me. Jesus said in Luke 15:4 that a good shepherd leaves 99 of his 100 sheep to find the one that is lost. You are lost this moment, but you *are* worth finding again!"

As Ingrid turned her red, swollen eyes into the kind, loving face of the pastor, Pastor Lewis felt his heart contract in his chest. Here was yet another hurting soul in a world already chock full of pain and misery. With someone so young, it was almost always an agony that did not have to happen.

Something inside Ingrid stirred. A tiny flicker of hope prompted her to let the elderly man pull her to her feet on shaky legs and half-carry, half-lead her into the chapel.

Inside it was fairly dark and cool. The peaceful setting was a slight balm to Ingrid's raw suffering. Pastor Lewis led her up the aisle and sat her down on the carpeted altar steps at the front of the church.

Sitting down beside her, he said, "Now then, Ingrid, please tell me what has you so upset that you think dying might be preferable to trying to work it out?"

"Oh!" Ingrid moaned, "I couldn't possibly tell you what I've done! I'm so ashamed!"

"You're hurting, child, and a wound can't heal without draining the infection. Please trust me, I'll not judge you or reprimand you—I only want to help you start your healing."

"Oh, pastor," Ingrid wailed as new tears began springing from her eyes, "I wish you *could* reprimand me and it was that easy! I could take the discipline and be done with it! But not this—now what I've done—I can either live with it forever or end it for good!"

Pastor Lewis said, "Dear one, prisons all over the world are full of people who, I'm sure, have done much worse than whatever you've done, and God can forgive them. He's waiting to forgive you also. He already knows what you've done, and if you'll only turn to Him in your sorrow, He *will* help you!"

The groan that came from Ingrid's mouth was so full of

grief that Pastor Lewis felt the sounds echo inside his rib cage. She cried out, "How I wish what you say was true! But you don't even know what I've done!"

Can I really make things right?

"Try me!" Pastor Lewis said confidently. "You know, if you can only let go and let yourself come to God you will be okay!"

Ingrid's entire body began trembling from deep inside her. As her rippling emotions surged outward, something snapped in her. She pressed her hands over her face and began to pour out her story to Pastor Lewis. Deep rage swelled within him as Ingrid gulped out how she had let herself be seduced by her want of love and acceptance into the the party world of drugs and sex. Pastor Lewis was enraged that so many contemporary young people found themselves in positions to have to deal with such pressures.

When Ingrid had finished telling her story by explaining that the stained-glass image of Jesus seemed to beckon her up the walk to the chapel, Pastor Lewis seized the opportunity.

"Yes, Ingrid, He did beckon you! And He's still trying to help you. He says straight out, 'Here I am! I stand at the door and knock. If anyone hears my voice and opens the door, I will come in and eat with him, and he with me.' He means you, Ingrid! Open the door to your heart and let Jesus come in to help you begin to heal."

"But, Pastor!" Ingrid wailed, "I knew that what I was doing was wrong! I knew I should have left the party from the moment I walked into the house! I didn't listen to my conscience!"

"Ingrid," Pastor Lewis said sadly, "you're not the first person to turn away from the Holy Spirit trying to counsel us to go in the right direction. And I've no doubt, however unfortunate, that you won't be the last. You have shattered a precious dream of youth—like millions before you—that people are either all good or all bad and as one of the good ones you are invincible to the bad ones' influence."

"I never thought I was invincible," Ingrid was quick to say, "but I *never* thought I'd fall into something like this—and so easily!"

"What you did last night involves some very unhealthy, destructive choices. Most people who have done similar things felt just as you do after the first time they were seduced by drugs, alcohol, and sex. You know, here is a key to why people *stay* involved in such ugliness—they feel so demeaned and degraded by what they've done that a sense of worthlessness takes over their self-image. That boy you were with last night—Gene—he was probably drawn into such activities much as you were, for similar reasons. But he may not have been walking by a chapel or felt Jesus beckoning to him afterward. Or possibly he did feel Jesus calling out to him but didn't recognize the stirrings, or else he chose to ignore them. It's very likely that Gene also felt it was impossible to be forgiven or correct his errors, just like you."

"Correct my errors?!" Ingrid couldn't believe Pastor Lewis. "You make it sound like I messed up on a test at school! Pastor, I messed up my whole life in one night! There's no correcting that!"

"Oh, yes, Ingrid, there is," Pastor Lewis said assertively. "You can use your experiences as valuable comparisons for how you do *not* want your life to be! You can use these things as mental guideposts to keep you away from such situations in the future! Why, even the apostle Paul spoke of the war going on within him between his mind and his body. But he assures us that even though we have sinful natures, they do not have to control us. We do not have to fear our sinful natures either, because if we believe in the Father, Son and Spirit, we are saved! We have the Spirit of God living in us and so we are free and can become more and more in control of ourselves!"

"Free?!" Ingrid nearly shouted. "Free?! I feel much more

trapped than free! Oh, just one night—and now look!"

"Many people say, 'If only I hadn't done that one thing'" Pastor Lewis replied. "What good does this do, Ingrid? The Bible says that 'all have sinned and fall short of the glory of God.' *All,* Ingrid, not some or many, but all! And in Romans 6:14 we are promised that 'sin shall not be your master, because you are not under law, but under grace.' Now, Ingrid, my task is to help you take control of your sins and become *their* master."

"If what you say is true, then why don't people just give up and live like savages—killing and stealing and whatever they want?" asked Ingrid, still filled with doubt.

"Because, just as Luke 16:15 says, 'God knows your hearts.' God knows what is in your heart, Ingrid. He judges by this! If someone kills, steals, lies, cheats, uses illicit drugs, or participates in immoral sex, then God knows if he is sorry, confused, ashamed, or grieving."

"So He knows—" Ingrid said. "What can I do about it?"

"Ah, that's a girl," Pastor Lewis smiled softly for the first time since finding Ingrid. "That is a productive, healing question! When you ask, 'What can I do about it?,' then you are headed in the right direction. And I'll answer you with another Scripture, Hebrews 10:22: 'Let us draw near to God with a sincere heart in full assurance of faith, having our hearts sprinkled to cleanse us from a guilty conscience and having our bodies washed with pure water.' Draw near to God, Ingrid, let Him forgive you so you can forgive yourself! Try to think of ways you can use this traumatic ordeal to help generate love and goodness in other people's lives."

"How do I draw near to God?" Ingrid asked, a shred of hopeful light shining within her.

"Start with 1 John 1:9. It promises, 'If we confess our sins, he is faithful and just and will forgive us our sins and purify us from all unrighteousness.'"

"Then what happens?" Ingrid asked with a growing, pleading hope.

"Then, Ingrid, by faith you can experience the greatest liberation you could ever dream of having! Second Corinthians 5:17 assures us, 'If anyone is in Christ, he is a new creation; the old has gone, the new has come!' You can start living all over, Ingrid! In Isaiah 1:18 the Lord says, 'Though your sins are like scarlet, they shall be as white as snow.' He means what He says!"

Ingrid felt seeds of hope begin to take root within her. The shroud of darkness that had encased her heart began to loosen its grip. She looked into Pastor Lewis's face to be sure of his sincerity. She saw only love and genuineness.

Pastor Lewis saw the penetrating look in Ingrid's eyes. He knew from many years of experience that she was at a turning point. Could she accept the poignant simplicity of God's all-encompassing ability to forgive, forget, and love? Or would she continue to punish herself unnecessarily when her painful experiences could be transformed into a vehicle for becoming a better person?

"Pastor Lewis?" Ingrid's voice quivered with emotion.

"Yes, Ingrid?"

"You know, I must tell you something. My father is a pastor, too, but in all my life I've never heard him give so much life or meaning to the Scriptures. I guess I've always thought of the Bible as a stuffy old book for old people."

Pastor Lewis reached out and patted Ingrid's hand, "Well, maybe you've just never been around when a young person needed your dad's help the way you needed mine today. The Bible tends to come alive for those who need its wellspring of guidance in times of crisis. If we'd just read this life-saving manual more often, and let it teach and comfort us, we'd save ourselves much grief."

Is suicide ever an answer?

"You've been a life-saver too, Pastor. To be honest, I was seriously considering going through with my threat of suicide."

Pastor Lewis's eyes filled suddenly with tears. In a near whisper he said, "I'm so glad you didn't, Ingrid. Six years ago next month my own daughter, Abbey, took her life. Believe me when I say that suicide is one of the cruelest, most self-indulgent ways that anyone can try to escape their problems."

Ingrid's heart bounded toward Pastor Lewis. She forgot her own misery for the moment. "Oh, I am so sorry! I didn't mean to hurt you!"

"No, no, dear," Pastor Lewis assured her. "Abbey's death spurred me on to a much deeper understanding of life's suffering, and it gave me an unquenchable desire to help ease that suffering whenever I can. This is one way I can pay tribute to Abbey's life."

"May I ask . . . " Ingrid hesitated.

"How it happened?" Pastor Lewis finished for her. He gazed off into space for a few seconds before he spoke again. "Abbey was our youngest child. She was about your age and also away at college. She was on her way home from a party late one night. She'd been drinking, ran a red light, hit a nurse who was driving home after picking up her infant son from the sitter's. Both the nurse and her child were killed. Abbey was charged with numerous things by the police and had to stand trial by jury for various reasons. Abbey saw the nurse's grieving husband and their two other children for several days in a row. Even though my wife and I, Abbey's three brothers and their wives were there trying to support her, Abbey couldn't deal with what had happened. Counseling didn't seem to help, and she just couldn't bring herself to a point of reconciliation. Like you, she thought she was so worthless that even God couldn't help her. Seven months after the trial, Abbey took an overdose of tranquilizers that her psychiatrist had prescribed for her."

The desolation in Pastor Lewis's voice and his body's defeated slump spoke more loudly than words ever could. She saw in these few, aching moments how futile, unnecessary, and destructive suicide really is. A life ended,

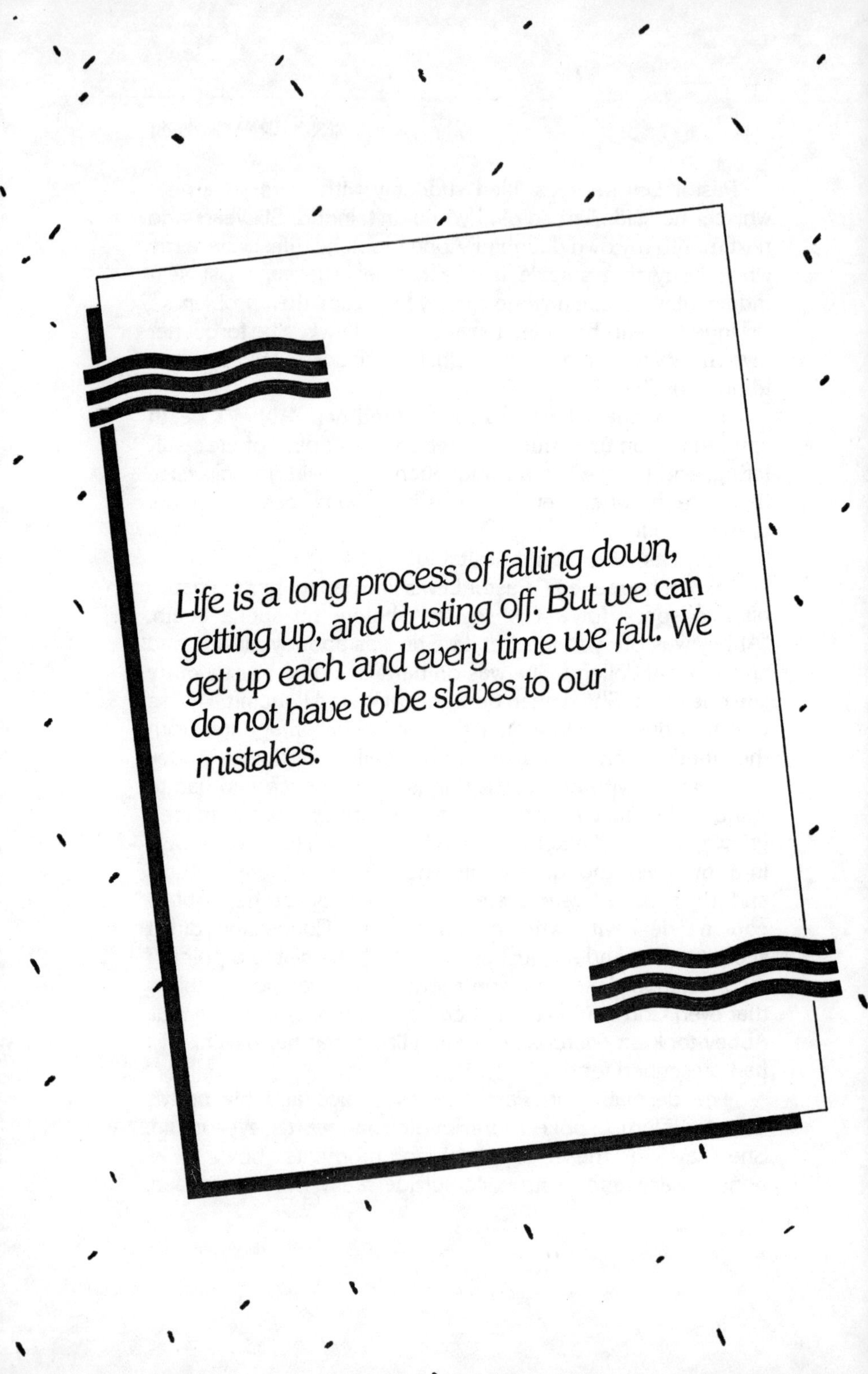
Life is a long process of falling down,
getting up, and dusting off. But we can
get up each and every time we fall. We
do not have to be slaves to our
mistakes.

others saddened forever, and permanent scars put on people's hearts with nothing good accomplished at all.

Pastor Lewis looked directly at Ingrid. "You know it is not God who causes life to become so painful that people choose to end it. It's people who choose to let life get that miserable. I don't hate Abbey for what she did to herself, but for a long while I resented that a poor choice she made one evening while partying could cause so many lives to be completely disrupted. Don't let that happen to you, Ingrid. Rise above the shame, disappointment, and heartache you're feeling over last night. Every day won't be perfect, and you won't get over this immediately.

Actually, life is a long process of falling down, getting up, and dusting off. But we *can* get up each and every time we fall. We do not have to be slaves to our mistakes! Isaiah 40:31 says, 'Those who hope in the Lord will renew their strength. They will soar on wings like eagles; they will run and not grow weary, they will walk and not be faint.' Hope in the Lord, Ingrid, in all areas of your life. You can go on and renew your heart, develop healthy friendships and relationships, and a well-adjusted attitude about your sexuality again. As long as you draw breath on earth, God offers you another chance to start anew."

Ingrid's experience may be much worse than what you will ever be involved in. On the other hand, you may be involved in the dark side of behavior and sexuality as deeply as she was. You may not think that God will understand the problems you face. But He does! All of the things which Pastor Lewis told Ingrid about confessing your sins, drawing near to God, forgiveness, love and even much more are *true* and *right!* Do not be afraid of God—draw closer to Him!

Healthy individuals and healthy couple relationships don't just happen, they are nurtured. They are possible because they are the natural plan of God! Life is not supposed to be a depressing experience. It should be a loving, gratifying journey and a joyful walk with God! In John 10:10 Jesus tells us plainly why He came into this world: "I have come that they may have life, and have it to the full."

Maybe you are in trouble right now—confused, hurting or doubting that you can ever make your life right again—turn to the back of this book to the "Where to Get Help" section. *Please* call one or more of the numbers to get you started on a life path that will help you solve your present problems, develop the skills you need to make better choices in the future, and enjoy the rest of your life to the full!

* * * *

An issue that causes much pain and heartache for many teens today is pregnancy. Teen pregnancy can seem devastating to the couple involved and their families. But this problem, too, *can* be worked out with careful, loving support. A big temptation for lots of "good," decent kids, however, is to arrange an abortion.

Is abortion the answer?

The desperation of an unwanted pregnancy can make abortion seem the easiest solution. It can seem like the only way to erase a mistake—to take it back. But a certain fact must be faced: There is *no way* to erase a pregnancy! The aftermath of abortion can be an emotional cloud of guilt, shame, and despair that follows you for years—or even for a lifetime.

Sixteen-year-old Linny undoubtedly needed to seek the advice of a stable adult to help her decide what to do about her pregnancy. But she didn't. She took care of it on her own and had an abortion.

Linny was left all alone to live with the shattered pieces of her heart. She thought her life was ruined. To make matters worse, she happened to see a preacher speaking on television against abortion one weekend. He was quoting Psalm 139:13-

16, "for you created my inmost being; you knit me together in my mother's womb. I praise you because I am fearfully and wonderfully made; your works are wonderful, I know that full well, My frame was not hidden from you when I was made in the secret place. When I was woven together in the depths of the earth, your eyes saw my unformed body. All the days ordained for me were written in your book before one of them came to be."

Linny's spirit was crushed with remorse as she heard the preacher's words. "Oh, God!" she cried, "I am sorry! I didn't mean to get in this mess!" She rocked back and forth repeating, "I didn't mean to. I didn't mean to."

Poor Linny. She was betrayed by her own panic and fear. Unfortunately, Linny kept her abortion hidden from her parents and other adults who could have helped her. That weekend she was so upset by hearing the preacher that she didn't listen to the rest of what he had to say—the part about God's complete forgiveness and unconditional love.

There just isn't anything you can do that would make God withhold His love from you! Drugs, sex, swearing, pregnancy, or abortion—they aren't problems that are too big for God! But, *you also need to ask an adult for help when you're in trouble!*

If you can't go to your parents, then go to a teacher, counselor, neighbor, coach, other relative, pastor, or doctor. They *will* help you! There may be pain and heartache as you confront your problem head-on, but it will be nothing compared to living with the despair, guilt, and shame of holding your sorrows inside. Get them out! Confess to God, ask His forgiveness and accept His help! His help probably won't be an immediate "letting you off the hook." It will more likely be a process of struggle and growth. But one day you will look back on your trouble and know you are a better person for facing it and working through the anguish. This is the courage and perseverence that good character is made of!

Let's put abortion in the context of other temptations

some teens may face. See how you feel about the way a few other teens handled some temptations of their own.

How do you bear up when you're facing temptation?

Read each situation below. Circle the number that corresponds to how you feel about it, using these responses:

1. I can really relate to that—I'd do the same or similar in that situation.
2. I cannot understand how anyone could do such things—I'd never react that way.
3. I don't really know how I would handle it if I were in this circumstance.

1. Betsy's parents told her that she had to be home right after the Spring Formal dance. Most of Betsy's friends had permission to attend an all-night, well-supervised party and breakfast at a local health club after the dance. She was extremely disappointed and angry about having to come home so early. To top things off, Betsy had been dating Wyatt for a few weeks and was very attracted to him. He would be at the festivities with the other kids all night. The more Betsy thought about having to tell Wyatt that she couldn't go on to the health club after the dance, the more frustrated and resentful she felt. Finally, she devised a plan to deceive her parents. She told them that she was staying with her best friend, Lisa, the night of the dance because Lisa couldn't stay late either. Betsy's parents were only too happy to accept this as a "solution" to Betsy's unhappiness over their restriction against the all-night party. Betsy did stay with Lisa the night of the dance and party—but Lisa had permission to stay out until the next morning. And Betsy stayed, too.

How do you feel about what Betsy did? 1 2 3

2. Jared was driving his father's new sports car one Friday evening. His dad allowed Jared to take the car only because he had a really special date. The young couple went to a very nice restaurant for dinner and had a wonderful time together. Afterward they went to a late movie. Jared brought his date home around midnight and kissed her gently at the door. It had been a perfect night. As he was pulling away from the curb he was thinking more about how great he was feeling than where he was driving. He scraped the side of the car that was parked in front of him and was sickened to see that his dad's new car had an ugly scratch. Jared looked quickly at the other car. He couldn't see any damage—only paint from his dad's car on the bumper. Jared swallowed a lump in his throat, quickly wiped as much paint as he could off the other car's bumper, got in his dad's car and drove away. All the way home Jared struggled with what to do—should he confess or make up something? His stomach was full of butterflies and he was sweating like crazy as he pulled his car into the garage. He barged into the house and told his dad that someone had hit the car in the parking lot of the movie theater and left the scene.

What do you think about what Jared did? 1 2 3

3. Marla's parents were very proud of her achievements on her school's swim team. She had broken records since joining the team in Junior High. In her senior year of high school, however, Marla began dating Troy. They fell deeply in love and Marla decided she wanted to quit the swim team so that she could spend more time with Troy. When she brought this up at home, Marla's parents were outraged. They yelled and screamed and asked her how she could sacrifice something that had been so important to her for nearly six years. They said that they were more disappointed in her than they had ever been. Marla was crushed. She ran from the room sobbing that her parents cared more about her public achievements

than they did about how she felt inside. After a few days of loud arguments and tearful displays of emotion, Marla agreed that she would stay on the swim team. Actually she quit. She let her parents believe she was still going to practices. Instead, she would go somewhere with Troy. When it came time for a swim meet, Marla would either have a mysterious "leg injury" or somehow confuse the dates and times so that her parents would miss the competition.

What do you think about how Marla handled this? 1 2 3

4. Stacy found out she was pregnant the week after her 17th birthday. She went to her boyfriend, Derek, right away. Both Stacy and Derek were in a state of panic. What should they do? They knew they didn't love each other enough to get married. Neither one was willing to get tied down to parenting. They thought their parents would "kill" them if they found out. Stacy couldn't bear to think of carrying a pregnancy to term and then giving a baby away for adoption. Besides the emotional agony, Stacy was in complete turmoil to think how it would be to try to cope with pregnancy most of her senior year at high school. The young couple decided that Stacy would get an abortion. Derek told his parents he needed a certain amount of money to buy materials for a project he was making in woodshop. Stacy went to the bank and secretly withdrew money that was supposed to be left alone as a college fund. One morning both Derek and Stacy faked calls of illness to the attendance office and drove to a suburban clinic away from where they lived. Stacy had an abortion and Derek drove her home at the same time she would normally arrive from school. No one ever knew about the abortion except Stacy and Derek.

How does this situation make you feel? 1 2 3

5. Brandon's first love is football, above everything else—

girls, school, parents, socializing, or his future. He has played football since he was seven years old. School and good grades have never come easy. In his sophomore year of high school, the varsity football coaches approached Brandon to move up and play on their team instead of the junior varsity. Of course he was elated. This was a high school dream come true for him. In order to get an opportunity to play for the varsity, however, Brandon had to work and train extra hard. His grades began to fall. Just before the semester ended, he discovered that unless he did very well on final exams, he would not have a high enough grade point average to stay on the team. He was devastated. He went to one of the assistant coaches and said he didn't know what he was going to do. The coach suggested a tutor and told Brandon how to contact one. Brandon's tutor was totally frustrated after the first three tries to help Brandon study. She told him in exasperation that the only way he was going to get good grades on anything was to cheat! Brandon considered this for several days and then made a plan to do just that. He enlisted the help of a friend who managed to slip him answers on every single exam. Sure enough, he made the grades he needed to stay on the football team.

How do you feel about Brandon's cheating? 1 2 3

Discussion

Obviously, every one of these kids did something that was morally wrong. They lied and cheated. They were tempted to save their own necks and get their own ways. Temptation is a very powerful motivator. Many good, decent people find themselves doing things that they wouldn't ordinarily do for the sake of avoiding unpleasant consequences, to get something they really want, or to save face in front of others. These pressures can be especially tough when it comes to teen pregnancy. For instance, Stacy gave in to the temptation to try to escape facing her pregnancy by having an abortion. But she forgot that abortion doesn't take away the consequences of being pregnant—it only shifts painful circumstances from one area to another.

Abortion alters the very process of creating human life. It can bring on a period of mourning—right afterward, months, or even years later. Feelings of loss, grief, and separation anxiety are very traumatic to anyone—young or old! If you are considering what to do about a pregnancy, bear in mind that:

1. Abortion is *not* an easy way out.

2. There may be supportive adults among your family and friends who would help care for you and your baby. Don't underestimate how much your parents love and care about you!

3. There are hundreds, even thousands, of Christian couples who long to adopt children. If you choose to give up your baby, you are choosing not only life, but most likely love, for this child! (You can learn about the choices and alternatives there are to abortion by calling one of the numbers in the "Where to Get Help" section in the back of this book.)

We have all fallen to temptation at one time or another. When we do, it is important to remember that we can turn to God, confess our sins, ask His forgiveness, and change our behavior. It is vital to know that the more we give in to temptation the easier it becomes. We may get so deep into self-indulgence, and try so hard to escape paying the consequences of our actions, that we separate ourselves from a peaceful relationship with God.

You are human. You may closely identify with and relate to what some or all of the kids above did. You may understand the agony of making the choices they made. Use these situations to think through how you face temptations in your personal life, and what you can do to help yourself from falling too deeply into the trap of letting go of your self-control. Discuss these circumstances with classmates, parents, or teachers, and see how they may have handled things differently, letting them know your reactions. And remember: God never allows you to be tempted beyond what you can bear, or without giving you a way to escape (read 1 Cor.10:13)! In fact, God believes very much in your ability to be good, strong leaders who can hold up under the pressures of growing up! As the apostle Paul told his younger friend, Timothy: "Don't let anyone look down on you because you are young, but set an example for the believers in speech, in life, in love, in faith and in purity" (1 Tim. 4:12).

As you step out into life it is inevitable that you will have problems—everyone does. You will have challenges to meet, stumbling blocks to avoid, and goals to achieve. Behind you, every step of your way, is a loving God who will help, protect and strengthen you. He doesn't want you to be fearful, lonely, confused, or ashamed. Go to God immediately when you do something wrong. Tell Him you're sorry and go forward, knowing it's taken care of by the highest Authority!

When you do fall down, make a mistake, or otherwise feel burdened, look to Philippians 3:13-14, where Paul says, "One thing I do: Forgetting what is behind and straining toward what is ahead, I press on toward the goad to win the prize for which God has called me heavenward in Christ Jesus."

During the rocky moments of life, when you have done wrong or been wronged, try to forget what's already been done and look joyfully toward tomorrow. You're a capable, meaningful person and you know what's right and best for you—you can feel it inside yourself! One way to help insure that you reach your best is to learn how to set positive goals for yourself. We'll look at how to do just that in the next chapter.

CHAPTER TEN

Getting Where You Want to Go

Some people think that setting goals applies only to things like college, careers, and athletic achievements. Not true! Goal-setting can help you get through *every* area of your life! In this chapter we will learn how to make goals and achieve them in a clear, step-by-step manner. You may want to keep a special "Goal Notebook," in which you can refer to your goals often and check on your progress toward them. As you see yourself meeting goals you've set, you may be amazed at how great you feel about yourself and how much confidence you begin to gain in your abilities.

Written goals can be particularly helpful during your teen years when you could otherwise lose sight of them in the day-to-day shuffle of your emotions. When you feel painfully depressed one day, and as though the whole world is yours the next, it can be extremely difficult to keep clear sight of your

goals. When you write things down and can look at them in black and white, they somehow become more objective—part of your life that is outside any inner turmoil you may be experiencing.

Despite all the turbulence of the teen years, they can also be some of the most wonderfully free and exciting years of your life. Setting goals for yourself as you go along is one way to help you get the most you can out of the last part of your passage into adulthood.

You only go through your teen years once. You will most likely never again undergo anything near the intensity and erratic fluctuation of your emotions during any other single segment of your life. Setting goals for your personal desires for self, school, future, friends, home life, sexuality, and couple relationships can help you get through your teen years with minimal upset and maximal happiness.

The following system can help you to devise a goal plan in any area of your life. You can follow these three steps again and again, regardless of how small or large your goals are:

1. *Examine where you are right now in any area of your life.* For example, you have no money and no car.
2. *Now think about where you want to get to.* In this example you may want to get enough money to pay for a car, the insurance, gas, and upkeep.
3. *Next you can list the best ways for you to get to where you want to be—not necessarily looking for the fastest or easiest ways to get what you want, but the best ways for you and anyone else who may be closely involved in your life.* For instance, to get the money to pay for a car and related expenses, stealing one or selling drugs may be the fastest way. But there is no question that these are *not* the best ways for you. Rather, thinking of ways to become employed, save money, and keep enough coming in to pay your way is best.

Eric is 18. He's wanted to date Sally for quite a while. Reading over a few of the pages in his "Goal Notebook" may help you get started on one of your own (see next page).

Sometimes you may make a clear goal-plan and then the going gets tough for you in another area of your life. You may have to temporarily set aside a particular goal-plan. But you can still look at your written lists and see that *you* are still moving along toward other goals in your "Goal Notebook." This can help you to stay calm and keep growing when there are complications in one area of your life or another. You can always come back and pick up a goal-plan where you left off.

For instance, shortly after Eric made his plan regarding Sally, he got into a real bind with keeping his grades up high enough to continue playing for the football team. For several weeks he had to put off his goal to get together with Sally and really hit the books. Every night after football practice, and on the weekends when he wasn't working his regular job at a local restaurant, he studied and did school work. But when all of his teachers had given him satisfactory reports on his grades, he was able to relax a little.

Eric looked at his "Goal Notebook" one evening and was reminded that he was only past the first step in his plan to get together with Sally. But he *had* already found out about her classes and extracurricular interests from a friend of Sally's older sister.

This way of discovering what you want to know—whether in personal relationships or business—is often called *networking.* Remember it! Networking is an invaluable means of helping you to achieve goals at every stage of your life. Everybody needs other somebodies to help us live safely, happily, and successfully in this world. By starting to develop your networking skills now, you do yourself an excellent favor.

Eric set to work on getting to the second item on his goal plan—to find mutual interests. This was easy for him because Sally was an athlete like himself. Sally went out for basketball, golf, and helped coach an elementary school tennis team.

1. Where I am right now: It's Fall; I want to date Sally.

2. Where I want to be: I want to have several dates with Sally, and know if we hit it off by Christmas vacation.

3. The best ways to reach my goal:

   a. Find out from mutual acquaintances what classes and extracurricular activities Sally's involved in.

   b. Pick a couple of activities that I'm interested in, too.

   c. Ask a mutual friend to invite both Sally and me to a group gathering or to introduce me to Sally.

   d. Find out some of the places where Sally usually goes at certain times where I can be sure to run into her. Check out schedules for her classes, work, church, or any lessons or practices.

   e. Strike up a conversation with Sally by asking her about topics I know we're both interested in.

   f. If the conversation goes smoothly, then ask Sally to get together for an event that involves our mutual interests, like a basketball game, art exhibit, or music concert.

   g. Follow through on this date. Try to branch out into a second area that we both already know we like, or one we discover on the date... stuff like kinds of food we like, sports, music, etc.

   h. Follow through on another date.

   i. If all is going well, then expand the time we spend together doing several things we both like. If we aren't hitting it off well, then cancel this goal.

Eric decided he would ask Sally to go on a date to play miniature golf.

The third thing on Eric's list was a stumbling block for him. He didn't know how to actually get introduced to Sally. The source of his information about her was too far out in his network to get him invited to a gathering where both Sally and he would be. Eric decided he would *brainstorm* ways to meet Sally on his own.

Brainstorming is another vital tool to remember for every area of your life! It simply means to come up with as many creative ideas as you possibly can to best achieve a goal. You may already have experience with brainstorming. No idea that you think of should be excluded from an initial list of ways to get to where you want to be! What seems like a wild, impossible idea at first may become the best way to do things, or maybe it can be modified to suit your purpose.

Eric took a separate page in his notebook and wrote the heading: "Ways to Meet Sally." Then he numbered his ideas:

1. Call her on the phone
2. Go up to her at school
3.

Now Eric was stalled. It wasn't basketball, golf, or tennis season, so he couldn't hang around after any practices to introduce himself. He wasn't sure enough of himself to simply telephone Sally, and they didn't have any classes together at school. This left the five minutes between classes in the hallway, or after school.

Eric decided to watch for a couple of days. With little trouble he passed Sally's locker on his way out of school the next day. The second time by, he heard Sally call over her shoulder to a friend that she had to hurry because she'd be late for play practice. This was the lead-in Eric needed. One of his friends had a small part in the holiday season play that their school put on every year and he would know about Sally.

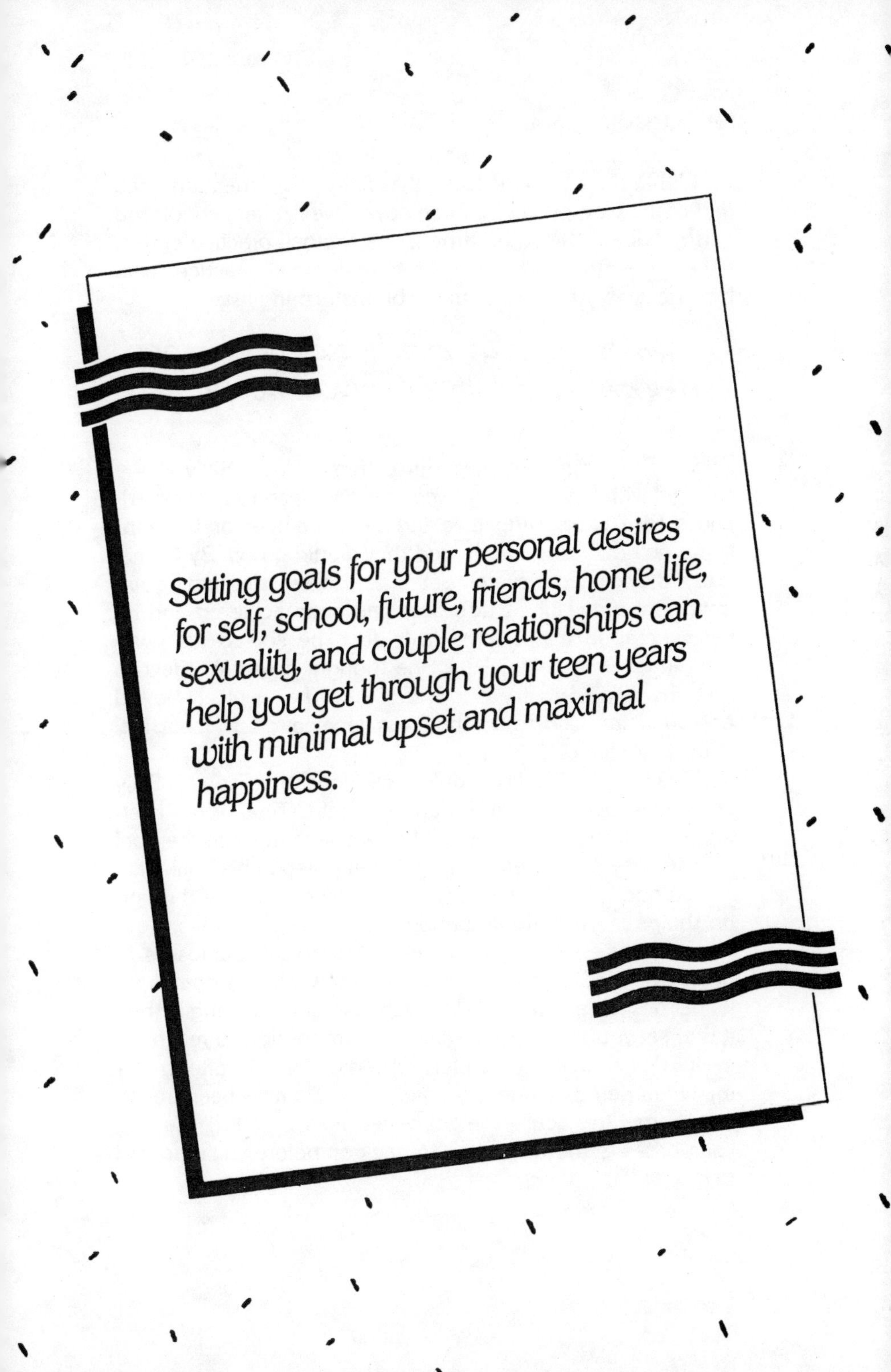
Setting goals for your personal desires
for self, school, future, friends, home life,
sexuality, and couple relationships can
help you get through your teen years
with minimal upset and maximal
happiness.

Within the week Eric knew that Sally had a medium-sized part in the play, practiced three days a week after school, and finished about the same time Eric's football practice ended. Except on Fridays. Eric didn't have football practice then. Now he knew what to add to his brainstorming list:

3. Watch the play practice on Friday and ask my friend to introduce me to Sally.

For Eric, things worked out extremely well. Sally was a nice girl with lots of energy and she was open to new experiences. By Thanksgiving, Eric and Sally had been on the miniature golf date Eric had hoped they would go on. By Christmas, they'd had several dates and were developing an important friendship. Eric's goal had been achieved and he felt very good about himself. In fact, he shared his goal-planning method with Sally. She thought it was so effective that she wanted to try it too. Eric gave her a nicely-bound notebook for Christmas that was labeled on the outside, "Goals for Life."

This type of situation could have gone another way. Sally could have been a great disappointment to Eric, or not been interested in dating him at all. For whatever reason, the goal Eric set may have been scrubbed at any step in his goal-plan.

Even this, however, is a successful way to follow through on things in your life. Situations just can't always work out perfectly. It is essential that you learn how to cut your losses. In other words, it's more important to know when a goal is no longer desirable or feasible to reach, and quit pursuing it, than it is to set yourself up for a goal that's impossible to reach.

If Eric had been completely turned off by Sally after meeting her or going on one date, then he would have been free to say, "Forget this goal—I've got better ones to go for!" Cutting your losses is knowing when to back off before you're forced to give up!

How do I know when to back off?

There is a big difference between giving up and knowing when to back off. For example, if you quit the track team after tripping over a hurdle during a meet and coming in way behind the pack, then you're giving up. If you quit the team after receiving a serious knee injury, then you're most likely backing off. Likewise, if your goal is to be on the honor roll and you cancel your goal after flunking one test, you're probably giving up. But if you flunk a class one semester that was extremely difficult and don't make your goal for this time, you may only be backing off for now.

You may be familiar with a cliche that says in effect, "I'll hang in there with this goal to the end, even if it kills me." Well, it just may! Some people get into the bad habit of seeking a goal long after it should have been trashed.

For instance, a businessman might pour thousands of dollars into a business that has given every indication that it's not going to make it, long before he finally gives up. By that time he may be completely broke, depressed, or divorced. He should have backed off while he was still healthy.

Learn how to cut your losses. You can develop a goal-plan and brainstorm how to do this too! If you need to back off from a couple relationship, a class at school, participation in a sport, a job commitment, or anything else, you can follow the same goal-setting formula by thinking through and writing down:

1. Where am I now?

2. Where do I want to get to?

3. What are the best ways for me to get there?

This formula, of course, applies to goals regarding your sexuality also.

Should I make plans and goals regarding my sexuality?

Many people get the impression that planning for their sex life is "wrong" or distasteful. They live with an invisible code that says, "If sexual feelings aren't expressed spontaneously, then they won't be fully enjoyed." This is quite fascinating when you consider how carefully we learn to plan for our personal hygiene, physical health, clothing styles, home decors, vacations, college majors, job changes, financial portfolios, and social schedules. Why would we plan our sexual choices with any less care? However, it is obvious that hundreds of thousands of people are very careless when it comes to planning for, making choices about, and expressing their sexuality. Planning, choosing, and expressing are vital keys in every area of life. We all have a sexual aspect in our personalities. Whether that sexual aspect is expressed through celibacy or activity, it is a part of a person's whole self.

Regardless of what you see in the media, or even what you hear from liberal-minded adults, your sexuality is a private part of yourself—just as your thoughts, feelings, tastes, ideas, and beliefs are. You cannot grab onto your sexuality like you can grab an arm. Sexuality is not a body part to be covered or exposed. Your peers, parents, pastors, and teachers cannot plan or choose *for* you how you will express your sexuality. The choice is *yours.* Others can plan *with* you or *help* you to make choices, but in the end—it's your life!

Many people seem to think that they *fall* into love with another person, and that expressing themselves sexually together is a by-product of their love which they cannot control. It would seem that people who think this way may also believe that if they fell into a bear trap the inevitable by-product would be death. Sound ridiculous? Of course it does! In the first place, a person would try to avoid falling into a painful trap. In the second place, if he did fall into one he would, of course, want to do whatever he could to try and escape it.

Your common sense may be screaming, "Not me! I would never get pulled into a trap—sexual or otherwise—because I know what I'm doing! I have self-control and the power to make good decisions! I'm not afraid, and I know about real love!"

If your reaction to warnings about dangers in your life are similar to these, then you're absolutely right! Second Timothy 1:7 tells us exactly this: "For God did not give us a spirit of timidity, but a spirit of power, of love and of self-discipline."

You are wonderfully made by God (Psalm 139:13-14). God doesn't want you, a wonderful person, to be trapped, afraid, helpless, unloving, or out of control. He wants you to express your love, plan your life courageously, and choose to be in control of your future. Sexuality is a wonderful part of your whole self. You can process the same plans, choices, expressions, and goals regarding your sexuality that you do in any other area of your life.

If I choose to remain abstinent or to stop having sex, what can I expect?

Risks regarding sexual activity, temptations, pressures, unresolved negative feelings, worries, and yearnings regarding your sexuality have been discussed throughout this book. For now, to help you make healthy choices for yourself, let's look at a college-age couple who has dated for three years and chosen, individually and together, to remain sexually abstinent while expressing their love in ways other than by having sexual intercourse.

Jason and Beth are nearly through their junior year at a state university. They met at a dorm party during the fall of their first months at college. Although they each dated other people off and on that first year, they shared a mutual feeling of magnetism toward each other and have gone together exclusively the last two years.

Jason readily admits that their choice to remain abstinent is an extremely difficult goal to keep their sights on. He says, "Holding back from having sex, especially when you love someone, is probably one of the biggest challenges any young, healthy couple can face. Of course Beth and I would like just to say, 'What the heck! We love each other and we're going to go for it!' But, if we do, we both give up on our goals for our future. By giving in, we'd take all the risks that go along with sexual activity—physically, spiritually, and emotionally—and lose sight of the emphasis we really need to place on other areas of our lives right now."

Beth adds, "Being together sexually is a natural, intensely pleasurable result of a loving, healthy relationship. I know that because of how good it is for Jason and me without having sex—things could only be better! I think one of the hardest things for a young couple about waiting for sex is that the half of us that's grown up is experiencing sexual thoughts and physical urges—that half wants sexual gratification right now! But the other half of us hasn't experienced enough life to fully grasp the risks of falling into a sexual relationship. The struggle to remain abstinent can become *very* complicated! Have you ever been working at a computer when, all of a sudden, strange new things you've never seen before come on the monitor? It's almost as if the computer has a life of its own! But when you think about it sensibly you know that a computer can only work with the input it is programmed to use. That's kind of like the two halves of a teen—wanting to use new information that hasn't been fully programmed yet."

"I don't know, Beth," Jason says, "look around us. We've said before that it's not just teenagers who struggle with this. It's sad, but we've grown up with some terribly poor input from today's society, as far as examples are concerned. Loot at the divorce rate! It tells you that about half of all couples have such major problems that they can't or won't work them out.

I'm not saying they all have to do with sexuality, but look at how many of our friends have sex now because they say, 'Why wait? Marriages don't last anymore anyway!' So many young couples look to adults and see how messed up their lives are and figure it's hopeless to set their standards so high. They think that life is only guaranteed for the day or night they're experiencing at the moment."

"Yeah," Beth agrees, "but I think that's a cop-out. What about the couples who *do* stay married and have happy lives? They set a good example to look up to."

"I know that," Jason says. "But look at all the stuff going on that has to do with sex directly. Movies, television, songs, adultery among public figures, pornography, and groups who want to legalize prostitution are constantly pushing sex in our faces. Plus, there's also all the gadgets, clothes, books—so many other products that are marketed with sex. It can look like the whole world is full of sex-crazed teens *and* adults! And we're only human. Evan if we choose to remain abstinent, we're still vulnerable to all the stimulation around us. A guy tends to think he's not normal if he's *not* thinking about sex!"

"Jason," Beth responds, "I know it's difficult, but we're talking about how to cope with difficulty and meet goals successfully! Anybody can think of reasons to give up, but what about reasons to keep going? What about the backbone of why we chose to stay abstinent in the first place?"

"Well, that's why we have our list, remember?" Jason grins.

"Yes," Beth smiles back, "I remember."

Jason explains. "You see, when we decided to be abstinent we made a list of reasons why we chose to wait for sex until we're married. Then we ripped the paper in half. I keep one half in my wallet and Beth keeps the other half in hers. When things get really tough and we think about backing out of our choice, one of us will bring up the list. Then we know it's time to put our two papers together and go over them."

"It probably sounds corny," Beth says sheepishly, "but it's really helped to ease the tension many times. Normally, we'll start out trying to get rid of our reasons and convince ourselves it'd be okay to have sex. Then it seems like one or another of the reasons will sort of jump off the page at us and we'll know it's right for us to wait. We usually end up laughing even if we are wistful about what might have been."

"It's funny though," Jason interjects, "whenever we've done this, there's something that clicks together and it's as if we're expressing our sexual tension in a different way. Laughing together is a natural high that helps to relieve the pressures of the moment."

Beth agrees, "That's really true. And our reasons stay more meaningful because we've grown closer and stronger as a couple. Our friendship keeps getting more important and our love gets deeper."

"Well, we might as well show the list since we're going into such detail," Jason offers. He takes a frayed piece of paper from his wallet and Beth takes one from hers. They put the two together. "It's easy to see they've been used a lot by how worn they are," says Jason, blushing.

What are some of the real risks of having sex outside of marriage?

Beth giggles nervously. "Okay, I'll read the reasons why we chose abstinence. We wrote down all the risks we'd take if we don't wait.

"1. We risk an unwanted pregnancy—*no* form of birth control is 100 percent safe!

"2. We risk dulling our ability to enjoy sex fully in our future marriage by always having the shadow of past experiences following us.

"3. We risk losing each other to doubt, mistrust, and disrespect—wondering if we've been with anyone before or will be later.

"4. We risk focusing too much attention on our sexuality

and losing sight of other things that need to be more important at this time of life—things like studies, friendships and developing our personalities.

"5. We risk missing out on getting to know each other as whole persons by paying too much attention to sensual things and not paying enough attention to the ideas, beliefs, sense of humor, tastes, goals, attitudes, talents, and abilities we each have to offer the world.

"6. We each risk losing our self-respect by giving up and not living up to our own expectations and standards.

"7. We risk the excitement of anticipation and preparation for our married sexual relationship.

"8. We risk getting so used to illicit sex that it becomes an abstract expression of our sexuality rather than a naturally fulfilling part of a healthy marriage.

"9. We risk feeling so guilty about having premarital sex that we love each other blindly and do not get beyond infatuation with each other to real love for the whole person.

"10. We each have a precious gift to offer our partner on a one-time-only basis when we get married. This will help us want to keep our marriage a one-time-only so we don't ruin a 'perfect' record.

"11. If we choose to have sex outside of marriage we are also choosing to go directly against God. We then grieve and disappoint Him, the Son, and the Holy Spirit (1 Thess. 4:3-8)."

Beth put the two pieces of paper down on a table near her and looked at them thoughtfully. "These are our reasons for not having sex before we're married," she says. "Pretty sobering, huh? But hopeful and exciting too! Any goal worth reaching is going to stretch us. While you struggle, though, you can keep anticipating the sweetness of victory!"

Jason nods, "Beth and I don't pretend to be perfect or able to breeze through this part of our life. That's why we use a list split in half. It's a tool to help us keep sight of and reach our goal. As far as I'm concerned, any goal that is successfully reached has been planned carefully and nurtured along one step at a time. People don't just wake up one day and find out they're out of control sexually. Usually they've made choices that undermine sexual abstinence instead of helping it along."

"Uh-huh," Beth agrees. "For instance, couples can choose to get drunk and make sure they end up parked alone at the end of an evening. Or they can choose to avoid alcohol and make sure they don't put themselves in a position when the night ends where they give in to temptation."

Setting goals and reaching them in every area of life involves courage, planning, self-control, self-respect, real love, determination, struggle, excitement, anticipation, and faith that the Holy Spirit will guide you every step of the way. John 16:13 says, "The Spirit of truth ... will guide you into all truth." And 1 Corinthians 9:24 says, "Do you not know that in a race all the runners run, but only one gets the prize? Run in such a way as to get the prize." Negotiating the passages into adulthood seems to require a lot of effort. But so does winning a race. Set your goals high, and go after them as though you are running a race . . . *to win!*

How close do you think you are to adulthood? This last quiz will help you think about getting where you want to go in a healthy, mature way.

Do you know how to get what you need/want in a way that's constructive for you and others?

Write the letter after each situation below that best corresponds with how you think you would react:

a. I would get revenge.
b. I would feel helpless to change things.
c. I would hold my feelings in.
d. I would say exactly how I feel—good or bad.
e. I would seek someone else's advice.
f. I would try to change things next time.

1. You are running first in a long distance track event. The next closest runner edges up on you. Just as he is making a break for the finish line, he bumps into you. You're sure he did this on purpose. You end up in fifth place.

How would you react? a b c d e f

2. There is a class you really want to get into at school. The school guidance counselor tells you that it's full and you're second on the waiting list. A few days later you find out that you got bumped into fourth on the list and three popular buddies have been allowed into the class.

How would you deal with this? a b c d e f

3. You are bested by a close friend for a part in the annual school musical. He gloats over his victory, and really rubs it in.

What would you do? a b c d e f

4. Someone cuts ahead of you in the lunch line.

How would you handle it? a b c d e f

5. A friend gets angry at you and tells you off in front of a group of peers.

How would you cope? a b c d e f

6. You really want to date a guy/girl that you've been attracted to for months, but you're terrified of rejection.

What would you do? a b c d e f

7. You interviewed for a job that you wanted and needed badly. When the interviewer calls, she says that you didn't get the position. She tells you it was a toss-up between you and another person.

How would you react to this? a b c d e f

8. Your parents ground you unfairly for something you didn't do. In order to convince them of your innocence you have to tell on your older brother. If *he* gets the same grounding it means he'll miss a special date that he's waited to go out on for weeks. Your brother's made it clear that he wants you to take the rap.

How would you handle it?   a b c d e f

9. A girlfriend has embarrassed you in front of a group by telling something that you told her in confidence. In fact, she's really making fun of you, and you were completely sincere when you confided in her.

How would you deal with this?   a b c d e f

10. Your neighbors have a daughter who's a real "bully." She's always ridiculing you, threatening to tattle on anything she can think of to get you in trouble and lying about you to the other neighbors.

What would you do?   a b c d e f

Tally Up!

If you marked anything other than *d, e* or *f,* then you may want to ask yourself how you can learn to be assertive in an acceptable way. Setting goals for yourself and reaching them always involves some combination of saying how you think or what you feel, getting advice from dependable people, and changing how you're doing things as you need to in order to constructively achieve your goals.

You cannot please everyone all of the time. Some people think that the "unselfish" thing to do is to put other people's needs first by always keeping their own desires to themselves or feeling helpless. It is not selfish to make your honest opinions and wishes known. It is not being a baby to make sure a guidance counselor knows that you aren't happy that he let another kid into a class in your place. It's not being a tattletale to expect your brother to pay his own price for doing something that calls for discipline. It's not too aggressive to let a potential employer know you'd like a second shot at a job because it really means a lot to you. There's nothing wrong with fair, healthy competition.

Use these situations as a starting point to discuss your ability to get what you want or need constructively. You may want to show this quiz to a teacher, youth group leader, your parents, or some friends and see how they would react to the circumstances. This may help you to see where you stand and how you may improve your assertiveness without becoming obnoxious. Some people think that to be assertive you have to be harsh or cruel. Not so! You can strive for what you want and need, while still being kind and compassionate. You can respect the feelings of others while still expressing yours.

You needn't tear other people apart or ridicule them in order to tell them what's on your mind. Be polite, be honest, and direct with what you have to say. Then, if others get upset, hurt, or angry, it's their problem to deal with instead of yours.

Use common sense, love, and care when you are dealing with others and you'll be all right! It's likely that you will put your own needs aside many times for the sake of saving other people's feelings, or because it's not the right time to go ahead. But don't worry—your time *will* come! Meanwhile, you do not need to be anyone's doormat.

It's a big world. There are so many wonderful people, places, and experiences that will come your way! You *can* make good choices for yourself—*now*—that are sound investments for your future happiness. You *can*enjoy your sexuality today while you prepare yourself to go joyfully into a marriage—as one-half of a loving, equal partnership—tomorrow. You *can* find love, goodness, and fulfillment in life! And you *can* step out with smiles in your heart, knowing that God is with you through the last part of your passage into adulthood.

Let me leave you with these encouraging words from Jesus: "*Do not be afraid, little flock, for your Father has been pleased to give you the kingdom*" (Luke 12:32).

Appendix

WHERE TO GET HELP

Action/Pride Drug Information Hotline	1-800-241-9746
Agency Information and Referral Service	1-800-621-3860
Be Sober Helpline	1-800-237-6237
Bethany Christian Services	1-800-238-4269
Birthright (Pregnancy Counseling)	1-800-848-5683
(in New Jersey call:	1-609-848-1818)
Child Abuse Hotline	1-800-422-4453
Child Find	1-800-426-5678
Cocaine	1-800-262-2463
National Adolescent Suicide Hotline	1-800-621-4000
National Center for Missing and Exploited Children	1-800-843-5678
National Pregnancy Hotline	1-800-344-7211
National Rape Hotline	1-800-222-7273

LOCALLY: Look in your Yellow Pages under "Counselors" and you will find a list of the types of counselors listed in your telephone book. Then turn to the specific kind you need.

You can also call a church, police station, hospital, school, or county mental health office to ask how to contact the kind of help you need.

When you or a friend are in trouble, the important thing is that you ask *somebody* for help. Even if you call your local library and ask them to look up a number or tell you who you might call in your area, you are on the road to changing a bad situation!

Remember what the Ultimate Source of help can do for you! In Mark 10:27 Jesus says, "All things are possible with God."

Notes

Chapter 1

1. "Kids: Sex and Choices," Community Television of California; KCET Journal with Robin Groth, April 9, 1988.

Chapter 2

1. Steve Rabey, "Helping 'Adult' Teens Face the Eighties," *Christianity Today*, February 19, 1988, p. 50.
2. Eve Belson, "Troubled Teens," *Orange Coast Magazine*, April, 1988, p. 65.
3. Ibid., p. 69.
4. Ibid.
5. Ibid., p. 71.
6. Ibid., p. 72.
7. Ibid., p. 74.
8. "Your Body and How It Works—Adolescence and Sexual Maturity." *The Columbia University College of Physicians and Surgeons Complete Home Medical Guide* (New York: Crown Publishers, 1985), p. 241.

Chapter 3

1. Adapted from: "The Private Life of the American Family," by Susan Jacoby; *Family Circle,* October 20, 1987, pp. 12,14,83,84 and 85. (Nearly 50,000 people, 18 and over, responded.)

Chapter 5

1. "Kids: Sex and Choices," Community Television of California; KCET Journal with Robin Groth, April 9, 1988.
2. "Study Shows Church Kids Are Not Waiting," from Josh McDowell Ministry Survey, "News" Section of *Christianity Today:* Washington, D.C., March 18, 1988, p. 55.

Chapter 6

1. Gary Smalley and John Trent, Ph.D., "Why Can't My Spouse Understand What I Say?" *Focus On the Family,* November, 1988, pp.3-4.

Chapter 8

1. Eve Belson, "Troubled Teens," *Orange Coast Magazine,* April, 1988, pp. 75-76.